VISUAL QUICKSTART GUIDE

MACROMEDIA CONTRIBUTE

FOR WINDOWS

Tom Negrino

 Peachpit Press

Visual QuickStart Guide

Macromedia Contribute for Windows

Tom Negrino

Peachpit Press

1249 Eighth Street
Berkeley, CA 94710
510/524-2178
800/283-9444
510/524-2221 (fax)

Find us on the World Wide Web at: http://www.peachpit.com/
To report errors, please send a note to errata@peachpit.com
Published by Peachpit Press, a division of Pearson Education, in association with Macromedia Press.

Macromedia Press Editor: Wendy Sharp
Editor: Carol Person
Copyeditor: Elissa Rabellino
Production Coordinator: Lisa Brazieal
Compositor: Kelli Kamel
Indexer: FireCrystal Communications
Technical Review: Erik Larson
Cover Design: The Visual Group

Notice of rights

Notice of liability

Trademarks

ISBN 0-321-16781-3

9 8 7 6 5 4 3 2 1

Printed and bound in the United States of America

*To my wife, Dori Smith, for her endless patience, her sharp
technical knowledge, and her boundless support and love.
"Smart chicks are hot!"*

Special thanks to ...

The folks at Peachpit

This project was like old home week, with all of the editorial and production people being former colleagues from *Macworld* magazine. It was like getting the band back together! Big thanks to the following:

Macromedia Press/Peachpit Press acquisitions editor Wendy Sharp, who brought me in on the project and who obviously doesn't hold *Macs for Kids and Parents*, which we wrote together so long ago, against me.

My editor, Carol Person, for her keen editing and patience with my foibles, and who is still a joy to work with.

Lisa Brazieal, the Goddess of Production.

Elissa Rabellino, for her eagle-eyed copyediting.

Everybody else

Web designer extraordinaire Suzanne Stephens, of Stephens Design (`www.stephensdesign.com`), who, with design assistance from Dave Stephens, her husband and partner, created many of the Web pages used as screen-shot examples in the book. If a Web page looks good, Suzanne did it. If not, it was my fault.

The people at Macromedia: Erik Larson, senior product manager for Contribute (and technical editor for this book); Eric Lerner, program manager; Ken Sundermeyer, Mr. Extensibility; Scott Unterberg; and Joann Peach.

My agent, David Rogelberg, of StudioB.

My son, Sean Smith, who put up with Cranky Dad with mostly good cheer.

Thanks to Endless River Adventures for their courtesy in allowing me to use their photos and their Web site as examples throughout this book.

The sound track for this book was graciously provided by Patty Griffin, Lucy Kaplansky, Alice Peacock, Bruce Springsteen, Richard Shindell, Lynn Miles, Warren Zevon, and, once more with feeling, the cast of *Buffy the Vampire Slayer*.

TABLE OF CONTENTS

Introduction   **ix**

Chapter 1:   **Getting Started**   **1**

Installing and Running Contribute 3
Exploring the Contribute Work Space 4
Getting Onscreen Help 9
Understanding Contribute's Workflow 10

Chapter 2:   **Making a Site Connection**   **15**

Preparing to Connect 16
Using the Connection Wizard 17
Sharing Site Connections 20
Importing Site Connection Keys 23
Editing Site Connections 24
Working Offline 25

Chapter 3:   **Building Web Pages**   **27**

Browsing Sites 28
Creating New Pages 32
Building New Pages from Sample Pages 36
Building New Pages from
        Dreamweaver Templates 38
Copying Existing Pages 40
Editing Existing Pages 41
Setting Page Properties 42
Setting Page Keywords and Descriptions 45
Editing Framed Pages 46
Saving Page Drafts 48
Letting Coworkers Review Your Pages 49
Publishing Your Pages 51
Rolling Back to Previous Page Versions 53
Printing Pages 54
Previewing Pages in External Browsers 55
Exporting HTML Pages 56

Chapter 4: | **Editing Page Content** | **57**
Basic Text Editing 58
Using HTML Styles 60
Using CSS Styles 69
Working with Lists 72
Inserting Dates 75
Adding Horizontal Rules 76
Inserting Special Characters 77
Finding and Replacing Text 78
Checking Spelling 80

Chapter 5: | **Working with Images** | **81**
Adding Images to Your Pages 82
Adjusting Image Properties 86
Editing Images 89
Adding Flash Content 94

Chapter 6: | **Working with Links** | **95**
About Linking 96
Linking to Draft Pages 97
Creating New Pages from Links 100
Linking to Web Addresses 102
Creating Email Links 104
Linking to Local Files 105
Adding and Editing Anchors 107
Editing and Removing Links 110

Chapter 7: | **Creating Tables** | **111**
Creating a New Table 112
Inserting Rows and Columns 119
Deleting Table Elements 121
Formatting Tables 122
Setting Table Properties 125
Merging and Splitting Cells 127
Setting Cell Properties 128
Sorting Table Contents 130

Chapter 8: | **Using Dreamweaver Templates** | **133**
Creating New Pages from
    Dreamweaver Templates 134
Dreamweaver Template Details 136
Working with Editable Areas 139
Setting Template Properties 141

Chapter 9:   **Working with External Documents**   **143**

Using External Documents 144
Importing Word or Excel Documents 146
Editing Imported Documents 150
Editing Other Document Types 151

Chapter 10:   **Site Administration**   **155**

Becoming an Administrator 156
Assigning Sitewide Settings 159
Assigning Permissions 165
Creating Permission Groups 174
Modifying Permission Groups 175

Chapter 11:   **Managing Sites with Dreamweaver**   **177**

Updating Dreamweaver for Contribute 178
Building Sites for Contribute 180
Enabling Dreamweaver Settings
      for Contribute 183
Sharing Connection Keys 185
Using Contribute Rollback in Dreamweaver . . . 187

Chapter 12:   **Customizing Contribute**   **189**

Understanding Contribute Extensibility 190
Creating Sample Pages Templates 193
Customizing the Welcome Screen 195
Customizing Menus 197
Changing Keyboard Shortcuts 199

Index   **201**

TABLE OF CONTENTS

INTRODUCTION

Welcome to *Macromedia Contribute: Visual QuickStart Guide*! Contribute brings a new approach to building Web sites, promising to make life easier for both Web designers and the clients who love them.

The World Wide Web has exploded from the simple sites of its humble beginnings in the mid-1990s, when building Web pages was easy, to today's large, complex Web sites, which require skilled Web designers to create them and programmers to make the pages work together and allow visitors to interact with the site. As sites have become more complicated, they have also become more fragile; designers and programmers are reluctant to let everyday users make changes and updates to Web sites for fear that minor mistakes will cause major problems.

At the same time, the Web has become a near-ubiquitous way for companies and organizations to get their message out. The irony is that the people who most need to be able to update Web sites quickly must go through their overworked Webmasters to have changes made. In most corporations, not a day goes by when someone doesn't complain that the Web team is taking too long to add a page, change a bit of text or an image, or make other requested changes.

continued on next page

And you can't blame the Web team for serving as gatekeepers, because it's too easy for inexperienced users to mess up the links on a page and break a site.

Macromedia Contribute allows designers to get back to the job of designing sites (rather than maintaining pages) and allows clients to maintain sites (rather than trying to track down the designers to make small changes). Best of all, everyone gets to do his or her job without worrying about breaking the site. With Contribute, anyone can safely make changes to Web sites.

What do you need?

To use Contribute, your computer needs to meet the following minimum requirements:

◆ A PC with a 300 MHz Intel Pentium II processor or the equivalent.

◆ Microsoft Windows 98 Second Edition, 2000, NT (Service Pack 3 or higher), Me, or XP (Home or Professional).

◆ Microsoft Internet Explorer, version 5.0 or higher.

◆ At least 64 MB of RAM.

◆ At least 30 MB of available disk space

◆ A color monitor capable of 800-by-600-pixel resolution and able to display 256 colors.

◆ One of the following email clients, a requirement for Contribute's email review feature: Microsoft Outlook, Microsoft Outlook Express, Qualcomm Eudora, Netscape Communicator, or Lotus Notes.

◆ A connection to the Internet (high-speed access is strongly preferred), or access to a Web server on a local area network (LAN).

As you can see, almost any PC manufactured since 1998 should be able to run Contribute comfortably. Contribute 1.0 runs only on Windows, though Macromedia has promised that it will release a version of Contribute for Mac OS X in 2003.

What I used

The screen shots used in this book were taken exclusively on a PC running Windows XP, with the exception of a few figures in Chapter 11, "Managing Sites with Dreamweaver" that show how you can use Macromedia Dreamweaver running in Mac OS X to administer your Contribute sites. Screenshots from any supported version of Windows should look pretty much the same as the figures in the book.

What's in the book

I've organized the different elements of building Web sites with Contribute into chapters, and within each chapter are step-by-step directions that tell you exactly how to accomplish various tasks. You don't have to work through the entire book in order, but it is structured so that the more complex material builds on the easier tasks.

Throughout the book I've included many tips that will help you get things done faster, better, or both. You'll also find sidebars (with gray backgrounds) that delve deeper into subjects. Be sure to read the figure captions, too; sometimes you'll find extra nuggets of information there.

My assumptions about you

Writing this book, I made the assumption that you're familiar with the basics of using Windows. You don't need to be a computer expert by any means, although you shouldn't be stumped by concepts like selecting text, using menus, clicking and dragging, and using files and folders.

If you're familiar with Microsoft Word and Excel, that will be helpful (especially when you get to Chapter 9, "Working with External Documents"), although it's not necessary. You should also be familiar with Web surfing and how to use Internet Explorer to view a Web site.

Even though you'll be using Contribute to add pages and content to Web sites, you don't need to be a Web designer, Web programmer, or Web anything. Heck, you don't even have to be a good typist.

There's more help on the Web

I've prepared a companion Web site for this book, which you'll find at:

`http://www.negrino.com/contribute/`

On this site, you'll find Contribute news, tips, tricks, and links to other online resources that will help you use Contribute better and more productively. If I discover any mistakes in the book that somehow got through the editing process, I'll list the updates on the site, too.

Let's get started

Macromedia Contribute is a new kind of software, one that allows people who don't want to have to deal with HTML, JavaScript, CSS, or any other Web technology to take their Web sites back into their own hands and get their thoughts and work onto the Web. It does this not by bypassing Web professionals but by forging partnerships with them. Contribute offers exciting possibilities for everyone who wants to express themselves on the Web.

So now, on with the book!

Tom Negrino

December 2002

GETTING STARTED

Welcome to Macromedia Contribute! With Contribute, you'll be able to easily add content to Web sites, with a minimum of hassle and complexity. You'll still need to know a little bit about how the Web works, but for the most part, as long as you can use a word processor (such as Microsoft Word), you'll be able to build Web pages with Contribute.

Contribute allows you to add new pages, text, images, Macromedia Flash animations, and more to your Web sites. With Contribute's built-in Web browser, you can view pages on your sites (or anywhere on the Web). On Web sites you are allowed to change, you can edit individual pages and then send the draft copies of those pages to your coworkers by email for approvals, or you can publish your changes directly to the Web site.

Contribute works hand-in-hand with Dreamweaver MX, Macromedia's powerful Web design program. Designers can create page templates in Dreamweaver, and those templates can then be used by Contribute. But Contribute isn't just friendly with Dreamweaver and other Macromedia products; it plays well with others, too. You can drag Microsoft Word or Excel documents into Contribute, and publish them easily and immediately on the Web. In fact, Contribute can work with documents from almost any other program.

In this chapter you'll learn how to install and run Contribute, and you'll get a look at Contribute's work space and user interface. Most important, I'll introduce you to Contribute's *workflow*, the sequence of events that let you create and edit Web pages.

GETTING STARTED

Figure 1.1 Double-click the Macromedia Contribute shortcut icon on your desktop to get started with the program.

Figure 1.2 Contribute's Welcome screen lets you learn more about the program, or lets you create a connection to your Web site.

Installing and Running Contribute

Like most programs, Contribute provides step-by-step instructions for installation as soon as you insert the CD-ROM into your computer. Here's a bit of guidance to help you get the application up and running.

To install Macromedia Contribute:

1. Insert the Contribute CD-ROM in your CD drive.

   The Contribute Installer automatically launches.

2. Follow the onscreen instructions to install the program.

   During the installation, you'll need to enter your serial number, which you'll find in the box; you can also get it from your site administrator if your company has licensed multiple copies of Contribute.

3. When the installation is complete, eject the Contribute CD-ROM.

   The Installer leaves behind a shortcut icon on your desktop (**Figure 1.1**).

To run Contribute for the first time:

If you are connected to the Internet, the first time you run Contribute, the program will prompt you to register with Macromedia. Since Contribute has a built-in Web browser, this is an easy process. After you finish registering, Contribute will display its Welcome screen (**Figure 1.2**).

The Welcome screen helps you learn about Contribute, and offers you a link to create a site connection. You'll learn more about creating site connections in Chapter 2.

◆ Double-click the Contribute icon on your desktop.

   or

   Choose Start > Programs > Macromedia > Macromedia Contribute.

Exploring the Contribute Work Space

In Contribute everything happens in one window; unlike other Web tools such as Dreamweaver, Contribute has no separate tool palettes, property inspectors, or other windows you need to manage. Instead, you get an uncluttered, clean interface (**Figure 1.3**).

Toolbar (in Browse mode)

Menu bar

Pages panel

How Do I panel

Sidebar

Document window

Figure 1.3 The Macromedia Contribute environment: The document window is in Browse mode, and the Browser toolbar is displayed.

The document window

Most of your work is done in Contribute's document window. You use the document window to browse to pages you want to edit. The document window works like any other Web browser; in fact, it is actually an embedded version of Microsoft Internet Explorer. You can use Contribute's built-in browser to view any Web page, but you can only edit pages in your own Web sites—that is, sites where you have editing privileges.

When you've browsed to the page in your Web site that you want to edit, clicking the Edit Page button in the toolbar switches the document window into Edit mode, allowing you to add or change text or graphic elements on the page.

✔ Tip

- Contribute's Web browser gets its preferences from your system's Internet Explorer browser. To change settings such as fonts or to enable plug-ins such as Flash or QuickTime, change the settings or install the plug-ins in Internet Explorer, then relaunch Contribute.

The toolbars

Contribute has two toolbars, the Browser toolbar and the Editing toolbar.

When you're in Browse mode, Contribute displays the Browser toolbar, which contains an abbreviated set of the familiar Web-browser controls, such as Back, Forward, Stop, and Refresh buttons, and an Address field, where you can type the URL of a page you want to browse (**Figure 1.4**). When you're browsing sites where you have editing privileges, the Browser toolbar also contains Edit Page and New Page buttons. When you're browsing sites where you don't yet have editing privileges, these two buttons are replaced by a single Create Connection button. Clicking this button starts up the process of making a site connection, which is required before you can edit the site. See Chapter 2, "Making a Site Connection," for more information. In some situations, the Browser toolbar may also show the *info bar*, which gives you more information about the page you're browsing.

Info bar

Figure 1.4 The Browser toolbar works just like Internet Explorer's, with the addition of the Edit Page and New Page buttons, and sometimes the info bar, as shown.

✔ Tip

- Blue text in the info bar is a hyperlink; you can click it to go to the page that the info bar is telling you about.

When editing a page, you'll see the Editing toolbar, which contains buttons and pop-up menus for common editing operations (**Figure 1.5**). Many of these controls replicate choices from the Insert, Format, and Table menus. You'll also see the Publish, Save for Later, and Cancel buttons, which allow you to publish the draft page you're working on to your Web site, save the draft for additional editing later, or cancel editing altogether.

Figure 1.5 The Editing toolbar contains tools to add and edit Web-page elements.

The sidebar

Contribute's main navigation tool is the *sidebar*. The sidebar also gives you quick access to brief tutorials on how to accomplish specific tasks. It has two panes:

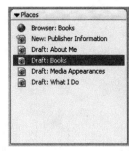

Figure 1.6 The sidebar's Pages panel allows you to switch between Browse and Edit modes, and lists new or draft pages.

◆ The **Pages panel** allows you to switch between the built-in browser and any new or draft pages you have open (**Figure 1.6**). When you click Browser in the Pages panel, you can browse to any page on the Internet, and that page is displayed in the document window. You can click any draft or new page listed in the Pages panel, and the document window switches to Edit mode and allows you to edit the page. Because all your editing operations in Contribute occur in the document window, the Pages panel takes the place of the Window menu found in many other Windows applications.

◆ The **How Do I panel** provides quick instructions to help you complete common tasks (**Figure 1.7**). The list of tasks changes, depending on whether you're browsing or editing. In either case, clicking a task displays more information on how to accomplish it (**Figure 1.8**). Some How Do I topics provide several layers of instructions; keep selecting until you get to the instructions you need.

Figure 1.7 The How Do I panel shows common tasks, for which it has step-by-step instructions.

✔ Tip

■ The Pages and How Do I panels are resizable. You can double-click the heading of either panel to collapse it, or you can drag the header of the How Do I panel up or down to adjust the size of either panel in the sidebar. Once you get used to using Contribute, you might want to collapse the How Do I panel altogether, especially to make room for new or draft pages in the Pages panel. You can also drag the border between the sidebar and the document to change their width.

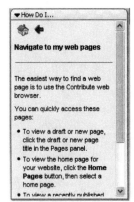

Figure 1.8 An example of Contribute's step-by-step instructions.

Figure 1.9 The Help menu gives you access to a variety of help and support resources.

Figure 1.10 To use Contribute's online help, you can either browse or search by keyword.

Getting Onscreen Help

Contribute's onscreen help is based on the standard Windows help system. Not surprisingly, you access the help files via the program's Help menu (**Figure 1.9**).

To get onscreen help:

1. Choose Help > Macromedia Contribute Help, or press F1.

   The Contribute Help window opens (**Figure 1.10**).

2. On the Contents tab, click the book icons to browse to the Help topic you want. The detailed documentation appears on the right side of the window.

   or

   Select the Search tab, type a search keyword, and click the List Topics button. The list of found topics appears in the "Select Topic to display" box. Click the topic you want, then click Display. The documentation appears on the right side of the window.

GETTING ONSCREEN HELP

Understanding Contribute's Workflow

In order to get the most out of using Macromedia Contribute, you need to understand how Contribute approaches the task of creating and editing Web pages. Other Web-site tools, even Macromedia's own Dreamweaver, are largely built around the concept that one person, or perhaps a team of people, has full access to a Web site, with the unfettered ability to make changes throughout the site. In contrast, Contribute presumes that one or more *site administrators* are responsible for managing a Web site, and one or more groups of users are able to add content to the site but have little or no need to deal with the site's design or its HTML or other code. For these content contributors, Contribute makes adding information to a Web site as easy as using a word processor such as Microsoft Word, but in part accomplishes this ease of use by limiting the ability of contributors to make design changes to the site.

The administrator's workflow

The Contribute administrator is responsible for setting up the connections to Web sites and defining what changes a user or group of users are allowed to make to the site. These *permissions* might, for example, allow a group called "Reporters" to create and edit pages, but not delete pages, a privilege reserved for the "Editors" group. Similarly, the "Copyeditors" group could be restricted to only editing text and changing its formatting.

Permission groups are created by the site administrator and distributed to the different user groups, via email or over a network, as part of a file called a *connection key*. The connection key, which is encrypted and protected by a password, contains the information the user needs to connect to the Web site over the local network or the Internet, and also contains that user's site permissions. To add the new site connection to his or her copy of Contribute, the user simply doubleclicks a connection key file. For more information on creating connection files, see Chapter 2. See Chapter 10, "Site Administration," for more information on setting up permission groups.

✔ Tips

- There can be more than one site administrator, and the administrative duties can be shared by a group.

- The site administrator can create a permission group that restricts editing to only specific folders. This is an especially useful capability because, for example, the administrator can keep the Marketing department out of Human Resources' Web pages, and vice versa.

- Administrators, by definition, have complete control over the Web site. The site administrator could also be one of the users, or perhaps the only user.

UNDERSTANDING CONTRIBUTE'S WORKFLOW

The contributor's workflow

As a contributor to a Web site, before you can begin editing pages, you must import or create a connection to the Web server. Most of the time, your Web-site administrator creates a connection key for you. To learn more about importing site connections, see Chapter 2. Once you've set up the site connection, there are three steps to editing any existing Web page in Contribute:

◆ First you **browse** to the page you want to edit using Contribute's built-in Web browser.

◆ You then **edit** the page using Contribute's editing tools. If you are editing an existing page, Contribute makes a draft copy of the page for you to work on. Contribute also locks the page so that no one can modify this page at the same time you're working on it.

◆ Finally, you **publish** the draft page to your Web site.

Understanding this **browse-edit-publish** workflow is the key to working with Web pages in Contribute.

Building new pages

Of course, you can also create new pages with Contribute, either from a new blank page, new pages based on *Dreamweaver templates*, or pages based on *non-Dreamweaver templates*.

Dreamweaver templates allow the page designer to create the page and designate portions of it as editable. The rest of the page is locked to the Contribute user. This ability to lock portions of a page is a great solution to the problem of users' inadvertently messing up page designs. The site administrator can specify which user groups have access to specific templates. When you create a new page from a Dreamweaver template, Contribute makes a copy of the template page and allows you to work only within the editable regions.

Non-Dreamweaver templates are pages that are completely editable and can be used as models for new pages. When you create a new page from one of these templates, Contribute makes a copy of the page, and you make your changes to the copy. As with Dreamweaver templates, the site administrator can specify user access. Contribute's Sample Pages are non-Dreamweaver templates. See Chapter 3 for more about Sample Pages.

UNDERSTANDING CONTRIBUTE'S WORKFLOW

MAKING A
SITE CONNECTION

2

Although it is possible to edit pages with Macromedia Contribute that are not on a Web server (this is called *offline editing*), chances are you will be using Contribute to create and edit pages over an Internet or local area network (LAN) connection to a Web server. The server could be the machine running your live Web site, sometimes called the *production server*, or it could be a test server, also known as a *staging server*. A staging server is usually used for editing and review of a site's pages where several people must approve the design and content before the site or page goes live on the Internet.

Regardless of whether you use a production or a staging server, you need to tell Contribute how to connect to the server before you can start working on pages. Contribute's Connection Wizard walks you through the connection process. Once you have connected to your Web site, you can use Contribute to create files called *connection keys*, which contain all the information needed to make a server connection with Contribute. You can share your connection keys with other people. All they have to do is import the connection key you send them, and they can connect to your site and start editing pages without needing to fiddle with connection settings themselves.

Preparing to Connect

Contribute can connect to your Web server in two ways. The more common connection, called *FTP* (see the sidebar "What's FTP?"), is used when your server resides on the Internet or on your company's intranet. The other way to connect is over your company's *local area network* (LAN).

Before you begin creating an FTP connection, you need to ask your network administrator for some information about the Web server you're using:

- ◆ Your name and email address
- ◆ The Web site address, which is usually in the form `http://www.mysite.com`
- ◆ The connection type, which will be either FTP or Local/Network
- ◆ The FTP address for your server
- ◆ The log-in name for the FTP server
- ◆ The password associated with the log-in name
- ◆ The folder's path on the FTP server that contains your Web site

Once you have all this information in hand, you're ready to use Contribute's Connection Wizard to set up your FTP connection with the Web site you'll be working on.

When connecting to a Web site using a Local/Network connection, you only need to know the location, or network path, of the folder that holds your Web site. You can locate the folder on your network using the Choose button in the Connection Wizard as described later in this chapter.

What's FTP?

If you've never done any Web-site maintenance before, you might be baffled by the term *FTP*. It stands for "File Transfer Protocol," and is a common method for transferring files (such as Web pages and images) between two computers connected to the Internet. Web servers often use FTP to send files between the server and the computer of whomever is maintaining the Web site. In order to do this, the server machine runs an *FTP server* program in addition to the Web server software. Normally you need a program called an *FTP client* on your computer in order to transfer files to and from an FTP server. Web page creation programs such as Contribute and Macromedia Dreamweaver have the FTP client functions built in.

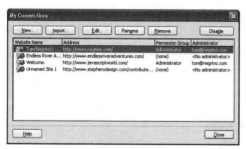

Figure 2.1 The My Connections window is where you manage all of your connection information.

Figure 2.2 In the User Information screen, you enter the name and email address for the connection.

Figure 2.3 Entering the URL of your Web site in the Website Home Page screen allows Contribute to find your site for editing.

Using the Connection Wizard

Connecting to a Web site can be a little intimidating, so Contribute provides an easy-to-use Connection Wizard, which walks you through the process. You can start the Connection Wizard by clicking the "Create a connection" link in Contribute's Welcome screen, which appears after you first install the program.

To make a site connection

1. Choose Edit > My Connections.

   The My Connections window appears (**Figure 2.1**).

2. Click the New button.

   The Connection Wizard starts up and displays a welcome screen.

3. Click Next. The User Information screen appears.

4. Enter your name, press Tab, then type your email address (**Figure 2.2**). Click Next.

   The Website Home Page screen appears (**Figure 2.3**).

5. Enter the address of your Web site. It's important to provide the entire Web address, so be sure to include the http:// portion of the address. Click Next.

continued on next page

6. You'll perform several steps on the Connection Information screen (**Figure 2.4**).

If you use FTP as your connection method, choose FTP from the pop-up menu and skip to step 9.

or

Choose Local/Network from the pop-up menu. The Connection Information screen changes to reflect your choice (**Figure 2.5**).

7. Click the Choose button next to "What is the network path to your website?"

In the resulting "Select Website Path" dialog, navigate to the location of your Web site in the usual Windows fashion.

8. Click the Next button, and skip to step 13.

9. Enter the FTP address for your server, then press Tab.

10. Enter your FTP log-in name, then press Tab.

11. Enter your FTP password, then click Next.

The FTP screen appears. There may be a delay before the FTP screen appears. This is normal; Contribute is verifying that the FTP information is valid. If there's a problem, an alert dialog will appear.

12. Enter the path to the folder on the FTP server that contains your Web site (**Figure 2.6**). Click Next.

This is where you are most likely to have problems, because the path that appears in a Web browser's Address line for a site is often not the actual path used by the Web server, which is what you need. Contribute will attempt to determine the right path to your site, but in some cases, you will have to enter it yourself. You'll need to get the actual path from your Webmaster or network administrator, or use the Choose button to browse to the correct folder.

Figure 2.4 Enter your FTP server information so that Contribute can upload and download edited files.

Figure 2.5 If you are editing pages on your local network, you must give Contribute the network path to the Web site.

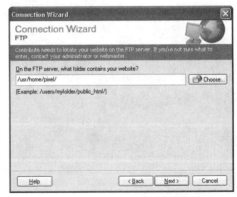

Figure 2.6 In the FTP screen you specify the folder on your Web server where your Web site resides.

Figure 2.7 In the Administrator Information screen you can designate yourself as the site's administrator.

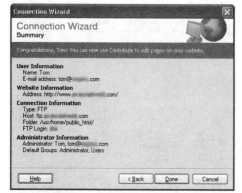

Figure 2.8 The Summary screen allows you to review the information you entered. I've blurred some sensitive information in this screenshot.

Missing Connections

You might have noticed that Contribute isn't as flexible as Dreamweaver at providing ways to connect to Web sites. Of Dreamweaver's six connection choices, Contribute does not offer four: None (Contribute requires that you edit pages on a server); RDS (Contribute can only edit pages residing on a ColdFusion server using FTP or Local/Network connections); SourceSafe Database (Contribute doesn't connect to databases); and WebDAV (Contribute does not yet support this protocol).

13. The Administrator Information screen asks if you want to become the administrator for this site (**Figure 2.7**). Select the Yes button, enter the administrator password for the site, and enter it again to confirm. This screen will only be displayed if no one has already set up Contribute administration for your site. Then click Next.

or

Click the No button, then click Next.

14. The Summary screen confirms that you have successfully made the connection, and summarizes all the information you entered (**Figure 2.8**). Click Done.

✔ Tip

■ You can set yourself up as the site administrator without an administrator password. Just don't enter anything in the password fields in step 13. A dialog opens, confirming that you really don't want an administrator password. The drawback to not having an administrator password is that any Contribute user of the site will be able to change the permissions for the site. See Chapter 10, "Site Administration," for more information on working with permissions and administering Contribute sites.

Sharing Site Connections

After you have created a site connection, you can save it as a file to your hard drive or email it to coworkers. Recipients of this *connection key* can import it into their copy of Contribute and immediately use it to make a connection and start editing pages without having to go through the connection setup process themselves.

Through Contribute's Permission Groups feature, you, as the site administrator, can limit the editing abilities of the recipients of your connection keys. Why might this be a good idea? Consider a situation in which you have a team (even a small team) working on a particular Web site, say a site for a community organization. You might want people assigned to update the News section of your site to be able to access pages only in the news folder, or you might want them to be able to modify existing pages but not create new pages. The Contribute site administrator can prepare and distribute different connection keys that specify the level of access allowed by team members. See Chapter 10 for more information about permissions.

To share a connection key via email:

1. Choose Edit > Administer Websites, then choose the Web site you want from the hierarchical menu. Contribute asks you to enter the site administrator's password (**Figure 2.9**).

2. Enter the password and click OK. The Administer Website window opens (**Figure 2.10**).

3. Click the Send Connection Key button. The first screen of the Export Wizard appears (**Figure 2.11**).

Figure 2.9 You'll need to enter the site administrator password to begin the sharing process.

Figure 2.10 Click the Send Connection Key button to start the Export Wizard.

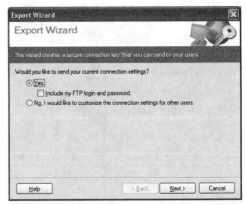

Figure 2.11 You can either send the connection file as is, or edit it before sending.

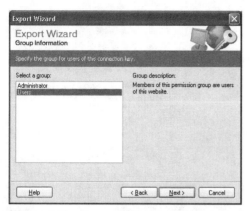

Figure 2.12 If you have specified permission sets, you can assign a set to the exported connection key.

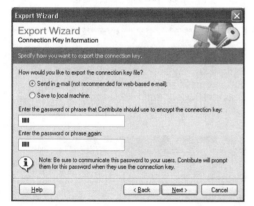

Figure 2.13 You can send a connection key file by email or save it to your hard drive, but either way, you must assign it a password.

4. Make sure the Yes button is selected, then click Next.

(Optional) Click the "Include my FTP login and password" checkbox.

If you want to include your log-in information in the key, check this; if the person you're sending the key to has his or her own FTP log-in, leave this option unchecked.

Note that if you choose No, Contribute will allow you to customize the connection settings before you create the export file. See Chapter 10 for more information about customizing connection settings.

5. The Group Information screen appears (**Figure 2.12**). Select the permission group you want for the connection file you're creating, then click Next.

6. The Connection Key Information screen opens (**Figure 2.13**). Choose whether to send the connection file in an email or save it to disk. Then enter the password or pass phrase for the connection file, repeat the password or pass phrase for verification, and click Next.

Contribute encrypts the connection key with the password or pass phrase so that it can't be opened except by the intended recipient.

7. The Summary screen of the Export Wizard appears, allowing you to review the information. If you need to make changes, click Back. Otherwise, click Done.

continued on next page

8. If you chose to send the connection key by email, Contribute launches your email program and create a new message with the connection key as an attachment, with the subject already filled in, and with instructions in the body of the message (**Figure 2.14**). Address the message, make any other changes you want, and send the mail on its way.

or

If you chose to save the connection key to disk, the Export Connection Key dialog appears (**Figure 2.15**). Choose the location on your hard drive or local network for the connection key, and click Save.

✔ Tips

■ You must enter a password or pass phrase to protect exported connection keys. Contribute won't allow you to create unprotected files.

■ If you email a connection key to a co-worker, you must make sure that he or she also receives the password or pass phrase for the file. But it will defeat the purpose of the protection if you include the password in the body of the email. Always communicate the password to the recipient in a separate communication, for example via fax, in a different email, or even by telephone. Shouting the password over cubicle walls is not considered to be a high-security solution!

■ Contribute uses your default email program, as set on the Programs tab of the Internet Properties control panel, to send email.

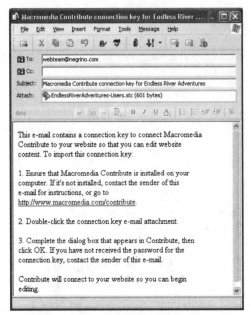

Figure 2.14 Contribute automatically creates an outgoing message in your email program (in this case, it's Microsoft Outlook Express), with the connection key file as an attachment.

Figure 2.15 Use the Export Connection Key dialog to save the file to your hard drive.

Figure 2.16 Use the Select Connection Key dialog to import connection keys to your hard drive and to open them.

Figure 2.17 To import a connection key, enter your name, email address, and password in the Import Connection Key dialog.

Importing Site Connection Keys

When you receive a connection key, you need to import it into Contribute in order to use the file and make the connection.

To import a connection key:

1. Choose Edit > My Connections. The My Connections dialog appears.

2. Click the Import button. The Select Connection Key dialog appears (**Figure 2.16**).

3. Navigate to the connection key on your hard drive, select the key file, and click Open or press [Enter].

4. The Import Connection Key dialog appears (**Figure 2.17**). If necessary, enter your name and email address, then enter the password or pass phrase for the connection key. Click OK.

✔ Tips

■ There's a faster way to import connection keys. Simply double-click on the connection key file which brings up the Import Connection Key dialog.

■ If you attempt to import a connection key and you already have a connection for that site listed in your My Connections dialog, Contribute asks if you want to replace the old settings file with the site settings you're importing.

Editing Site Connections

On occasion, you'll need to edit a site connection. For example, if you were to move your Web site from one Web hosting service to another, you would need to edit the connection to point to the new hosting service. You might also need to modify the connection if your organization began using a staging server; in that case, you would edit the connection to point to the staging server instead of the production server.

To edit a site connection:

1. Choose Edit > My Connections. The My Connections window appears.

2. Select the connection you want to edit, then click Edit.

3. The Connection Wizard opens. Use the Wizard to make any changes to the connection. If you need more information about using the Connection Wizard, see "Using the Connection Wizard," earlier in this chapter.

✔ Tips

- You can't duplicate an existing connection as a basis for a new connection. You must create the new connection from scratch.

- If you connect to the site using a connection key sent to you by your network administrator, the site connection information will be locked and you will only be able to change your user information. These sites will be identified in the My Connection dialogs with a globe and key icon as described in the "Connection Icons" sidebar.

Connection Icons

A close examination of the different connections in the My Connections window shows an icon next to the name of each Web site (**Figure 2.18**). Each of these icons tells you something different about the kind of connection:

- The icon with a computer and globe shows that the connection was created with the Connection Wizard.

- The icon overlaid with a key shows that the connection was created with a connection key.

- An icon with a slash through it indicates that the connection is disabled.

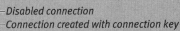
Disabled connection
Connection created with connection key

Connection created with Connection Wizard

Figure 2.18 The icons in the My Connections window signify how the connection was created.

Disabling Site Connections

Connection Disabling is a feature that tells Contribute not to pay attention to a site connection. When you disable a connection, Contribute won't let you edit or publish pages on the Web site, though you can still browse the site.

Connections are automatically disabled if a connection is no longer usable (for instance, if there is a network failure or if the Web server becomes unreachable for some other reason). You can also manually disable a network connection by choosing Edit > My Connections (**Figure 2.1**), selecting a Web site from the list, and clicking the Disable button.

One of the benefits of disabling a site connection is that Contribute starts up faster, especially if you have connections to several sites. When you launch Contribute, the program connects to all of the enabled Web sites and ensures that its copies of each Web site's templates are identical to the current versions of those templates, as someone else might have updated the templates since the last time you worked on the site. The more enabled site connections you have, the longer the process takes. You can see that it would be beneficial to disable connections for sites you don't need to update very often, or if you're working with a slow network connection, such as a dial-up modem.

The easiest way to reenable a disabled connection is to browse to the site, then click the Retry Connection button on the toolbar.

Working Offline

Most of the time, you'll want to use Contribute while connected to your Web server, whether that Web server is on the Internet or elsewhere on your local area network. But Contribute also allows you to create new documents and edit existing draft pages when you're not connected to any network. This is called *working offline*.

To work offline:

1. Choose File > Work Offline.
   Contribute disconnects from the network.

2. You might now choose to edit any documents that appear under the Pages section of the sidebar or you can choose File > New Page.

To reconnect to your network:

◆ Click the Work Online button in the Edit bar.
   or
   Uncheck the Work Offline item in the File menu.

BUILDING WEB PAGES

Now that you've made one or more site connections, you're ready to take advantage of Macromedia Contribute's ability to Browse, Edit, and Publish pages to your Web sites.

Contribute gives you a wide variety of tools for creating and editing Web pages. You can build new pages from scratch; use Contribute's built-in Sample Pages; create new pages based on Macromedia Dreamweaver templates; or even copy existing pages on your Web site. You can also edit existing pages and their properties, and allow your coworkers to review your draft pages before you publish them to the site. If you make a mistake, you can even use Contribute to roll back pages to a previous version. In this chapter, you'll learn how to do all these things and more.

Browsing Sites

Contribute has a built-in Web browser (**Figure 3.1**). Actually, it's an embedded version of the Microsoft Internet Explorer Web browser that comes as part of Windows. You use this built-in browser to navigate to pages you want to edit. You can also use it just as you would most Web browsers, to view HTML pages on the Web or on your local network. The familiar Address bar is there to enter Web addresses, as are the Back and Forward buttons. You navigate to new pages by clicking links, just as in any browser. When your pointer hovers over a link, the link's destination address appears in the browser's status bar at the bottom of the browser window.

You can browse to any Web site with Contribute, but you can only edit pages on Web sites for which you have a connection key (see Chapter 2, "Making a Site Connection," for more information on connection keys). When you browse to a page on a site where you have permission to edit, the Edit Page button is enabled in the toolbar.

Contribute's browser is useful (and essential for working with your sites), but it doesn't always work the same way as a stand-alone browser; see the "Contribute Browser Limitations" sidebar for details. Still, it's easy to use and even has several shortcut keys to speed your browsing (see **Table 3.1**).

To browse to any Web page:

1. If necessary, click Browser in the Pages panel.

2. In the Address bar, type the Web address (URL) of the page you want to view.

3. Press ⌞Enter⌟.
   Contribute displays the Web page.

Edit Page   *Browser toolbar*

Status bar

Figure 3.1 Contribute's built-in browser allows you to navigate to pages you can then edit.

Table 3.1

Browser Navigation Shortcuts	
SHORTCUT	**WHAT IT DOES**
⌞Alt⌟-⌞←⌟	Back; returns to the previously viewed page.
⌞Alt⌟-⌞→⌟	Forward; displays the page you were viewing before you clicked Back.
⌞Esc⌟	Stops loading a page.
⌞F5⌟	Reloads the current page.
⌞Ctrl⌟-⌞O⌟	Displays the Go to Web Address dialog; equivalent to clicking and typing in the Address field.
⌞Ctrl⌟-⌞Shift⌟-⌞O⌟	Displays the Choose File on Website dialog, allowing you to select a file on one of the sites for which you have a connection key. Equivalent to clicking the Choose button on the toolbar.

BROWSING SITES

Figure 3.2 The Go To Web Address dialog presents another way of browsing to a page.

You can use another method to browse to a page:

1. Choose View > Go to Web Address, or press Ctrl-O.

    The Go To Web Address dialog appears (**Figure 3.2**).

2. Type the URL of the page you want to view.

3. Click OK.

    Contribute displays the Web page.

✔ Tips

■   There's a bug in Contribute that requires you to click OK in the Go To Web Address dialog; pressing Enter won't do the trick.

■   You can jump back to the browser at any time by choosing View > Browser, or by pressing Ctrl-Shift-B.

■   Bookmarks you create in Contribute (by choosing Bookmarks > Add Bookmark) also appear in Internet Explorer's Favorites menu, inside a folder called Contribute Bookmarks. Similarly, favorites you create in Internet Explorer appear in Contribute's Bookmarks menu, under Other Bookmarks.

■   If a page is taking too long to appear, click the Stop button in the toolbar to stop loading the page.

■   You can reload a page in the browser by clicking the Refresh button in the toolbar.

Contribute Browser Limitations

Contribute's built-in browser is an embedded version of Internet Explorer, but it doesn't have all of IE's capabilities. There are several things Contribute's browser doesn't do, or does in a different fashion than IE.

◆   Contribute's browser doesn't allow you to open more than one main browser window at a time. If, while browsing, you click a link that is set to open the resulting page in a new window, the new window will open in your computer's default browser (usually Internet Explorer). Oddly, Contribute's browser can sometimes open separate pop-up windows triggered by JavaScript.

◆   Most online shopping carts don't work in Contribute's browser. Use a stand-alone browser to do your shopping.

◆   The built-in browser also has trouble with many password-protected Web sites. So you probably should use a different browser to do your online banking and pick up your Web-based email.

BROWSING SITES

Browsing your sites

Contribute offers two tools on the Browser toolbar that help you navigate easily to sites for which you have established connections. The first tool is the Home Pages pop-up menu, and the second tool is the Choose button.

The Home Pages pop-up menu (**Figure 3.3**) contains a list of all the home pages for the Web sites you can edit. It's like a list of favorites that allows you to move rapidly among your Web sites.

The Choose button allows you to quickly find and browse to a particular file on one of your Web sites. Clicking Choose when you're not already displaying one of your sites brings up the Choose File on Website dialog, with all your sites listed (**Figure 3.4**). It's very easy to find any file on any of your Web sites this way, much faster than typing URLs in the Address bar, because you can navigate directly through folders to pick files. If you're already browsing one of the Web sites you can edit, clicking the Choose button brings up the Choose File on Website dialog already set to browse the files on that Web site. The Preview pane of the dialog helps you find things fast (**Figure 3.5**).

Figure 3.3 Jump quickly between your site connections with the Home Pages pop-up menu in the Browser toolbar.

Figure 3.4 The Choose File on Website dialog is the fastest way to browse to a particular file on one of your sites.

Figure 3.5 The Preview pane in the Choose File on Website dialog tells you if you have found the right file.

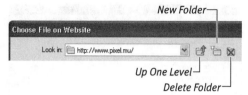

New Folder

Up One Level

Delete Folder

Figure 3.6 You can accomplish some useful navigation and file management with the controls at the top of the Choose File on Website dialog.

✔ Tips

■ The names of the menu items in the Home Pages pop-up menu are taken from the names of the Web sites in the My Connections dialog. You can edit the names in that dialog to make the menu items shorter or more descriptive.

■ You can also open the Choose File on Website dialog by pressing Ctrl-Shift-O.

■ The items at the top of the Choose File on Website dialog can help you with navigation and file management (**Figure 3.6**). The "Look in" pop-up menu allows you to move quickly among your different Web sites. If you've been digging deep into a site, the Up One Level button makes it easy to move up to the next level in the folder hierarchy. Using the New Folder and Delete Folder buttons, you can change your site's folder structure.

Creating New Pages

Most of the time when you're working with Contribute, you create new pages based on template pages—either the example pages that come with Contribute or templates created for you by your site's designers in Dreamweaver or other Web design and development tools. Creating new pages from templates is discussed later in this chapter.

Alternatively, you can create the page and create a link to the new page in one operation. In fact, that's how Macromedia recommends you create pages, so as to avoid orphan pages—pages with no link to them—on your Web site. See "Creating New Pages from Links" in Chapter 6 for more information.

Sometimes, though, you simply want to create a new blank page in one of your existing Web sites, and Contribute can do that, too.

To create a new blank page:

1. Browse to the Web site where you want to add a new page. It must be a site for which you have established a connection.

2. Click New Page on the toolbar.

   or

   Choose File > New Page, or press [Ctrl]-[N]. The New Page dialog appears. In this dialog, all your Web sites will be listed, but the site in which you're working will be expanded and Blank Web Page will be selected (**Figure 3.7**).

3. Press [Tab] to highlight the "Page title" box, and enter a title for your new Web page.

   This title will appear as the page's title in Web browsers.

CREATING NEW PAGES

Figure 3.7 When you're creating a new page using the New Page dialog, Contribute automatically selects the Blank Web Page for you.

✔ Tips

- Contribute considers a page to be a new page until you publish it to the server, even if you click the Save for Later button.

- The default filename Contribute provides in the Publish New Page dialog often has both upper- and lowercase text. It's better to manually change it to all lowercase; otherwise, your site's visitors will need to type in the exact filename in order to get to your page.

- Many alert dialogs in Contribute have a "Don't show again" check box. Once you get used to using Contribute, you might want to select these check boxes to speed your work.

- Contribute doesn't like pages without names; it won't let you create a new page until you give it a page title.

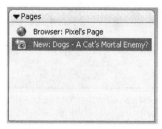

Figure 3.8 New pages are listed in the Pages panel of the sidebar.

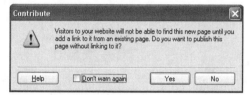

Figure 3.9 Contribute reminds you that if you don't create a link to the page you've created, visitors won't be able to find it.

Figure 3.10 You can accept the default filename Contribute gives you, but it's usually better to edit the filename so that it is all lowercase.

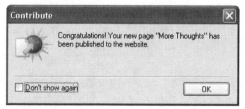

Figure 3.11 Contribute congratulates you on publishing your page.

4. Click OK.

Contribute creates the new page and lists it as a new page in the Pages panel (**Figure 3.8**). You may now add content to the page.

5. Click Publish to save the new page to your server.

If you haven't linked the new page to any other page, Contribute displays a warning dialog (**Figure 3.9**).

6. Click Yes or No. Remember, if you publish the page, you need to create a link to it if you want site visitors to find it.

7. Contribute displays the Publish New Page dialog, where you need to enter the filename for the new page (**Figure 3.10**).

The filename will appear at the end of the Web address for the page. By default, Contribute enters the filename as the page title with spaces removed and the filename extension .htm appended. If desired, enter your changes to the filename.

8. (Optional) If you want to save the new page in a folder on your Web site other than the current folder (which is the folder that contains the current page that is displayed in the browser). Click the Choose Folder button to open the Choose Folder dialog. Navigate to where you want to save the new page, and click the Select button.

The Publish New Page dialog reappears.

9. Click Publish.

Contribute publishes your new page to the Web site and displays a congratulatory dialog (**Figure 3.11**).

Contribute switches back to its browser and displays the newly published page.

Canceling pages

When you're editing a new page that you created, you can discard the new page by canceling it. If you're editing a draft of an existing page, canceling the draft page discards your changes and keeps the currently published version of the page.

To cancel a new or draft page:

1. In the Pages panel, select the new or draft page you want to cancel.

   Contribute displays the page in the browser window.

2. Click Cancel on the toolbar.

   or

   Choose File > Cancel Draft.

3. Click Yes when Contribute asks if you want to permanently delete your new page (**Figure 3.12**).

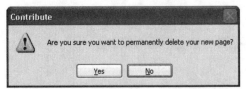

Figure 3.12 Are you sure you want to delete that page?

Deleting pages

You can delete Web pages or any kind of file from your Web site as long as your site administrator has given you file-deleting permissions as part of your connection key.

To delete a file from your Web site:

1. Browse to the page or file you want to delete.

2. Choose File > Delete Page.

   The menu item will be disabled if you don't have permission to delete pages on your Web site or if you have an unpublished draft of the page.

   Contribute displays an alert box asking if you're sure you want to delete.

3. Click Yes to confirm the deletion.

Building New Pages from Sample Pages

Contribute comes with 14 built-in sample Web pages you can use as templates for your own Web pages. You have a choice of three colors for most of the sample pages: Silver (the page elements are shades of a light gray), Forest (medium green shades), and Sky (darker blues), as listed in **Table 3.2**.

These sample templates make a good starting point for many pages. They aren't especially fancy, but they can help you get the job done quickly and will be all that some people need to whip out a page on deadline. The prebuilt calendar templates are especially useful.

To create new pages from sample pages:

1. Browse to the Web site where you want to add a new page. It must be a site for which you have established a connection.

2. Click New Page on the toolbar.

   or

   Choose File > New Page, or press Ctrl-N.

3. In the New Page dialog, click the small plus button next to Sample Web Pages.

   The four folders for the page categories— Business, Personal, Calendars, and Collaboration—appear.

4. Click the small plus button next to one of the categories to disclose its contents.

5. Select one of the Sample Web Pages to view it in the Preview pane (**Figure 3.13**). Below the preview is a short description of the template.

Figure 3.13 Contribute's Sample Web Pages are a quick way to get started building pages.

Table 3.2

Contribute's Sample Pages

CATEGORY	TEMPLATE NAME	COLORS
Business	General Content	Silver
	Two-Column	Forest
	Grouped Item List	Sky
	Home Page	
	Table Data	
Personal	Photo Album Page	Silver
	Résumé	Forest
	Multiple-Photo Album Page	Sky
Calendars	Generic Month	Silver
	Individual January 2003 through December 2004 calendars	
Collaboration	Project Home Page	Silver
	Meeting Notes	Forest
	Presentation Slide	Sky
	Report	

Figure 3.14 Sample Web Pages aren't especially pretty, but they are convenient.

6. Press Tab to highlight the "Page title" box, and enter a title for your new Web page.

7. Click OK.

Contribute creates the new page based on the template (**Figure 3.14**).

✔ Tips

■ Because of a bug in Contribute, you can't double-click folders in the New Page dialog to disclose their contents. Click the small plus buttons next to folders instead.

■ You can make your own Sample Pages and add them to the New Page dialog; see "Creating Sample Pages Templates," in Chapter 8 for details.

■ As with any page you create in Contribute, it's a good idea to create the new page and the link to the page at the same time.

Building New Pages from Dreamweaver Templates

Chances are, many of the pages you'll create as a content contributor will be based on templates created in Macromedia Dreamweaver MX. These templates will be created by your site's designer and will be made available to you by your site's administrator.

A Dreamweaver template can contain two types of regions. *Locked regions* cannot be modified by Contribute users. Examples of locked regions on a template might be navigation bars, some page backgrounds, and section titles. *Editable regions* are containers for content, which could include text or images, that can be changed by the Contribute user. Contribute shows you the editable regions on draft pages, outlined in green, with tabs for the names of each region (**Figure 3.15**).

This section of the book merely shows you the basics of creating pages from Dreamweaver templates. For more information, see Chapter 8, "Using Dreamweaver Templates."

To create pages from Dreamweaver templates:

1. Browse to the Web site where you want to add a new page. It must be a Web site for which you have established a connection.

2. Click New Page on the toolbar.
   or
   Choose File > New Page, or press Ctrl-N.

Locked regions

Editable regions

Figure 3.15 In this Dreamweaver template, the editable regions are shown outlined in green, with tabs for the name of each region.

—Locked regions   Editable regions—
with No cursor

Figure 3.16 The No cursor tells you where you can't edit.

3. In the New Page dialog, click the small plus button next to Templates.

The templates defined for your Web site appear.

4. Select a template to display it in the Preview pane.

5. Press ⟨Tab⟩ to highlight the "Page title" box, and enter a title for your new Web page.

6. Click OK.

Contribute creates the new page based on the template.

✔ Tips

■ Your Web-site administrator can designate any page on your site as a template, which will then be available in the Templates category in the New Page dialog. See Chapter 8, "Assigning Permissions," for more details.

■ The cursor turns into the international symbol for "no" (a circle with a diagonal slash through it) when you enter locked regions in Dreamweaver templates, indicating that you don't have permission to edit (**Figure 3.16**).

Copying Existing Pages

Most of the time you'll want to use templates with Contribute, but sometimes you might want to duplicate a lot of an existing page's content, and a simple copy, with a few changes, will do.

When you create a copy of a page, you must first create a new page, and subsequently make a link to it. Unlike most situations in Contribute where you create pages, here you cannot create a copy and add a link to it at the same time.

To make a copy of an existing page:

1. Browse to the page you want to copy.

2. Click New Page on the toolbar.
   or
   Choose File > New Page, or press Ctrl-N.

3. In the New Page dialog, click Copy of Current Page.
   The Preview pane shows you what the copy will look like.

4. Press Tab to highlight the "Page title" box, and enter a title for the new page.

5. Click OK.
   Contribute creates a new page that is a copy of the page you were browsing, and then enters Edit mode.

✔ Tips

■ You cannot create a copy of a page that contains a frameset.

■ You can only copy pages you're viewing with the Contribute browser; you can't make a copy of a draft page.

■ Unfortunately, you can't copy a page from one of your Web sites to another Web site.

Editing Existing Pages

By now, editing pages on your Web sites should be pretty clear. First you use the Contribute browser to view a page on a site you have permission to edit, then you enter Editing mode.

To edit pages in Contribute:

1. Browse to the page you want to edit.

   Use the Choose button in the browser toolbar to navigate to pages quickly.

2. Click the Edit Page button in the toolbar.

   or

   Choose File > Edit Page, or press Ctrl-Shift-E.

   The draft page appears in the editor, and the draft's title appears in the Pages panel in the sidebar.

✔ Tips

- You'll usually be connected to your Web site when using Contribute, but you can create new draft pages or continue editing existing draft pages (usually pages you created while working online) in Contribute's Offline mode. Choose File > Work Offline. Offline mode is especially useful if you're using a slow network connection, like a dial-up modem.

- Sometimes Contribute displays a message saying you can't edit a page because the page is being edited by someone else. If this happens, you might have to wait until the other person is finished with the page, or you can contact your site administrator.

Setting Page Properties

Page properties are settings that affect the entire page you're editing. They include the page title, background image or color, margins, default text color, and link colors.

You can change the page properties for any page you can edit unless the page is based on a template or you have been restricted to text-only editing by your site administrator. In those cases, you're only allowed to change the page title, and most of the options in the Page Properties dialog will be inactive.

To set page properties:

1. Browse to the page for which you want to set page properties, and then click Edit Page in the toolbar.

   Contribute creates a draft of the page.

2. Click the Page Properties button in the toolbar (**Figure 3.17**).

   or

   Choose Format > Page Properties, or press Ctrl-J.

   The Page Properties dialog appears (**Figure 3.18**).

3. Change the page title. The title you give your page will be displayed in the Web browser's title bar.

   or

   Change the page's background: Click the Browse button next to the "Background image." box. A menu pops up with two choices: Images on My Computer and Images on Website. Choose one of these locations to navigate to a graphic file you want to use as a background for the page.

Page Properties —

Figure 3.17 Use the Page Properties button on the toolbar to change page attributes.

Figure 3.18 The Page Properties dialog allows you to edit the page's title, change the background color or image, and much more.

Color box

Figure 3.19 Use the color picker to change the background, text, or link color.

or

Choose a link color: Click one of the color boxes. The color picker appears (**Figure 3.19**). Click on a color with the eyedropper to select it; the color can be any color in the picker or on your desktop. See the "Pick Your Link Color" sidebar for details.

or

Change the page's margins: Enter a value, in pixels, for one or more of the four margins of the page. Leaving a value blank is the same as entering zero.

or

Change document encoding for a non-Latin alphabet: From the "Document encoding" drop-down menu, select the character set for the page. You use this only when you'll be adding content in a language that uses a non-Western (non-Latin) alphabet. The default document encoding, Western (Latin1), is appropriate for English and Western European languages. Encodings are also available for Japanese, Chinese, Korean, Central European languages, Cyrillic, Greek, Icelandic, and Other. By setting the correct document encoding, you ensure that Web browsers can display the proper set of fonts to view your page.

4. Click OK to accept your changes.

✔ Tips

- Most of the time, a background image and a background color are mutually exclusive. If you select a background image for the page, your site's visitors won't see the background color.

- Use background images with care and delicacy. Chances are, you've seen pages where the background image obscured the content, making the text all but unreadable. Use subtle images.

- If you select a text color, it will be the default color for text on the page. That doesn't mean you can't change the color of selected text on the page. See Chapter 4, "Editing Page Content," for more information.

- Templates created in Dreamweaver maintain their document encoding when used in Contribute, so if you often need to create pages in non-Western languages, ask your site designer to build a Dreamweaver template with the correct encoding.

Pick Your Link Color

You can set colors for three kinds of links in Contribute: Link, Visited Link, and Active Link.

The Link color is the link's initial color before a user clicks the link. The default link color for most browsers is blue.

The Visited Link color is the color to which a link changes after a user has clicked the link and visited its destination page. For most browsers, the default color for visited links is purple.

The Active Link color is the color a link turns if a user holds down the mouse button after clicking the link. The standard default color for active links is red.

You can set alternative colors for any of these, but be aware that if you change them, it may be a bit harder for some users to navigate your site, because links may not appear as they expect. It's also not a good idea to set the same color for Link and Visited Link, because users won't be able to tell what parts of your site they've already visited.

Figure 3.20 Page keywords and descriptions help search engines find your site.

Setting Page Keywords and Descriptions

Page keywords and descriptions are bits of information that your site's visitors never see but are read by browsers and Internet search engines. Search engines use keywords to improve the accuracy of their search results. Some search engines also use descriptions to display the results.

Page keywords and descriptions are two types of special HTML tags called *META tags*. Meta-information is information about information; in this case, the keywords and page description are bits of information about the page itself.

To set page keywords and descriptions:

1. Browse to the page where you want to set keywords or descriptions, and then click Edit Page in the toolbar.

   Contribute creates a draft of the page.

2. Choose Format > Keywords and Description, or press Ctrl-Alt-K.

   The Page Keywords and Description dialog appears (**Figure 3.20**).

3. Enter your keywords in the Keywords field.

   Keywords in this field are separated by commas. You should try to use keywords you believe people would use when trying to find your site in an Internet search engine such as Google, AltaVista, or Yahoo! Search.

4. Enter your page description in the Description field.

5. Click OK to save your keywords and descriptions.

6. Click Publish to save your work to the server.

✔ Tip

■ If you want to see your keywords and descriptions, you need to open the page in an external browser such as Internet Explorer, and then view the page's source code. See "Previewing Pages in External Browsers," later in this chapter, for more information.

Editing Framed Pages

A Web page with *frames* is split into two or more rectangular areas, each of which has independent content. Frames are commonly used to define navigation and content areas for a page. The frame with the navigation area remains constant, and the content area changes when the user clicks a link in the navigation area. For example, many online shopping sites use frames to display their products in the content frame while allowing the user to browse to new content using the navigation frame. Frames can scroll independently, and the Web designer can even turn off scroll bars for particular frames.

When a user views a Web page that has been created with two frames, the browser is actually using three different files to display the page. In addition to the two frames the user sees, there's a third page, the *frameset* page. The frameset page is an HTML page that is invisible to the user but tells the browser how to display the frames and the pages they contain. It stores information about the size, location, and layout of each frame. Each frame within the frameset is a separate HTML file.

Contribute doesn't allow you to create or edit framesets, which must be created or changed in Dreamweaver or some other Web design tool, but it does allow you to edit any of the HTML pages within the frameset. In other words, you can change the content of any of the frames. Contribute does this by opening the HTML page that makes up the frame as a draft page.

When you browse to a page that has frames, the individual pages that make up the frames can come from the same or even different Web sites. You can edit content in any frame in which you have permission to edit.

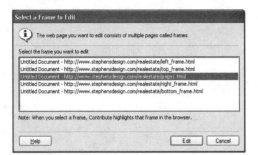

Figure 3.21 Choose the frame you want to edit.

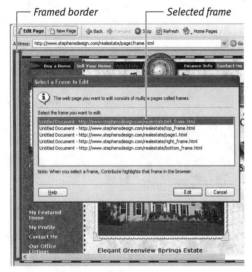

Framed border   *Selected frame*

Figure 3.22 Selecting a frame in the Select a Frame to Edit dialog puts a border around that frame in the editing window.

To edit content in a frame:

1. Browse to the page with the frames you want to edit.

2. Click the Edit Page button.

   Contribute displays the Select a Frame to Edit dialog (**Figure 3.21**). This dialog contains a list of all the frames that make up the page (but does not include the frameset page). The list includes the page titles and URLs for each of the frame pages.

3. In the dialog, select the frame you want to edit.

   Contribute puts a thick red border around the frame you selected, which helps you confirm that you have chosen the correct frame (**Figure 3.22**).

4. Click Edit.

   Contribute opens up the frame page as a new draft page, without the other frames.

5. Make your edits.

6. Click the Publish button to save your changes to the server.

✔ Tip

■ Normally, when you have a draft page open, and you switch back to the browser and view the published version of the page, Contribute shows, in its message area directly below the Browser toolbar, that you have an unpublished draft of the page you are viewing. For some reason, Contribute doesn't do that when you have a draft of framed page.

Saving Page Drafts

One of the nice things about Contribute is that although you can save draft pages manually, you'll hardly ever need to. Contribute saves your work automatically in the following situations:

◆ Whenever you switch to the browser

◆ When you switch to another draft page

◆ When you publish the current draft page

◆ When you choose File > Publish As New Page

◆ When you exit Contribute

If you want to save draft pages manually, you can do so by choosing File > Save, or by pressing Ctrl-S.

✔ Tips

■ Contribute performs most of its automatic saving when you switch from one page to another. Therefore, it's probably not a bad idea to hit Ctrl-S from time to time when you create a large amount of content for a particular page in Contribute, just to make sure your work is preserved in the (let's hope unlikely) event that Windows or Contribute crashes.

■ If any of the frames in the frameset have been marked by the page designer as noneditable areas, these frames will appear in gray text in the Select a Frame to Edit dialog, and won't be selectable.

Figure 3.23 When you send a page for review by email, Contribute apprises you of the process.

Letting Coworkers Review Your Pages

It's fairly common to have your boss or other coworkers review your draft pages before you publish them on your Web site. Contribute allows you to notify coworkers via email when a draft page is waiting for their review. One of the beauties of this review process is that recipients don't have to have Contribute, or Dreamweaver, or any other Web design tool; all they need is a Web browser and the ability to receive email.

When you make a draft available for review, Contribute does two things:

◆ It creates a temporary copy of the draft page on the same server where you publish your Web site. This temporary copy can't be edited by the reviewer.

◆ It creates an email message in your default email application (which is usually Microsoft Outlook or Outlook Express) that contains a Web address pointing to the temporary copy of the draft page.

After viewing the temporary copy of your draft page, the reviewer should send you his or her feedback in an email. You can then make changes to the draft page in Contribute. After that, you can either send the changed draft for additional review (repeating the review process) or simply publish the draft page.

To send a draft page for review:

1. In the Pages panel of the sidebar, select the draft you want to send for review.

The draft page appears in the editing pane.

2. Choose File > Email Review.

Contribute displays a dialog that describes the review process (**Figure 3.23**).

continued on next page

3. Click OK.

Contribute takes a moment to create the temporary copy of the draft page on the server, then launches your email application and creates a new message (**Figure 3.24**). The new message has a subject automatically inserted, and the body of the message contains a link to the temporary copy of the draft page.

4. Address and send the email message.

After the mail has been sent, Contribute uses the message area below the toolbar to inform you that you posted the draft for review, with the date and time (**Figure 3.25**). There is also a link that allows you to view the draft version you sent for review.

✔ Tips

■ If the page being reviewed is part of a frameset, the review address is for the single page you edited, not the entire frameset.

■ When you publish or cancel the draft you sent for review, Contribute deletes the temporary copy of the draft it placed on the server for the reviewer.

■ If for some reason Contribute cannot open your email application, you can still create the email message by clicking the Click Here link in the message area under the toolbar. The temporary copy of the draft page appears in the browser. Copy the URL for the temporary page from the browser's Address bar, and paste the address into an email message.

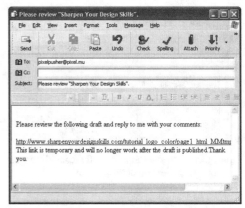

Figure 3.24 The page-review announcement email in Outlook Express.

Figure 3.25 After you send a page for review, Contribute reminds you in the message area below the toolbar.

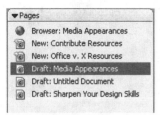

Figure 3.26 The two new pages will be published when the selected draft page is published, because the draft page contains links to both the new pages.

Figure 3.27 Edit the filenames for the new linked pages.

Publishing Your Pages

When you've finished editing a draft, you're ready to publish it to your Web site for the world to see. If you are publishing an update to an existing page, Contribute replaces the current version of the page that is live on your Web site with the new version.

Because it is possible for you to create links to new, previously unpublished pages as you work on a draft page, Contribute also publishes those new pages when you publish the current draft page; otherwise, you would have a page on your Web site with links to nowhere (**Figure 3.26**).

To publish page updates:

1. In the Pages panel of the sidebar, select the draft you want to publish.

2. Click Publish.

   If the draft page doesn't have links to any new pages, Contribute simply publishes the draft to your Web server. But if the draft contains links to any new pages, the Publish New Linked Pages dialog appears (**Figure 3.27**).

3. For each of the new pages, edit the filename and choose the folder where you want the page to reside on your server.

   Note that Contribute displays the Web address for each of the new pages.

4. Click Publish All.

✔ Tip

■ The default filename that Contribute provides in the Publish New Linked Pages dialog usually contains both upper- and lowercase text. Change the name to all lowercase to make it easier for site visitors to type the page's URL and easily reach your site.

Publishing existing pages as new pages

The equivalent of Save As in Contribute is its ability to make changes to an existing page and then publish it as a new page. Unlike simply publishing a draft, publishing an existing page as a new page doesn't overwrite the existing page.

To publish an existing page as a new page:

1. Browse to an existing page on your Web site.

2. Click Edit Page.
   Contribute creates a draft of the page.

3. Make your changes to the draft.

4. Choose File > Publish as New Page.
   The Publish As New Page dialog appears (**Figure 3.28**). If you haven't linked the new page from an existing page, Contribute displays a warning. After you publish the new page, you should create a link to it from one of the other existing pages on your Web site.

5. Change the page title and the filename for the new page.
   If you don't change the filename, Contribute automatically changes it for you so that you don't accidentally overwrite the existing page when you publish it.

6. Click Publish.

Figure 3.28 When you publish an existing page as a new page, you'll need to edit the filename for the new page in the Publish As New Page dialog.

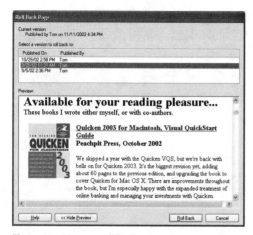

Figure 3.29 You can roll back a page to any previous version, up to the limit the site administrator set for you (in this case, that limit was three versions).

Rolling Back to Previous Page Versions

Contribute has the ability to *roll back* published pages—that is, revert to previously published versions of the pages. Think of it as a sort of "Super Undo" for your Web sites. You can roll back to the last published version, or to any saved version.

Contribute can roll back to "only" 99 versions of a given page, but your site administrator will probably limit you to far fewer rollbacks.

To roll back to a previous page version:

1. Browse to the page you want to roll back.

2. Choose File > Roll Back to Previous Version.

   Contribute gets the version information from the server and displays the Roll Back Page dialog (**Figure 3.29**).

3. From the list of page versions at the top of the dialog, choose a previous version.

   Contribute displays the page in the Preview section. If it's not the version you want, select another.

4. Click Roll Back.

   Contribute replaces the currently published version of the page with the previously published version.

✔ Tips

- When you roll back a current version of a page to a previously published version, the current version is saved on the server as a rollback version, and you can revert back to it.

- Site administrators can enable or disable rollback for groups of users. See Chapter 10, "Site Administration," for more details.

- As long as you have the ability to edit a page, you can roll it back. Contribute doesn't restrict rollbacks to the person who last edited or published the page.

- The Roll Back Page dialog is resizable, so you can preview more of the rollback version.

Printing Pages

Now that we have all reached the nirvana of the paperless office, there's never any need to print pages. All right, I admit I'm dreaming. You might want to print your pages for review by people who aren't online, for the boss who never quite got the hang of this newfangled Web thing, or simply because sometimes you can see errors on paper faster than you can see them on-screen. Contribute allows you to do a print preview before you print a page.

To preview and print a page:

1. Browse to the page you want to print.

2. Choose File > Print Preview.

   The page appears in the preview window (**Figure 3.30**). You can change the page's magnification to get a closer look.

3. Click Print.

✔ Tip

■ If you don't want to preview a page first, you can simply choose File > Print.

Figure 3.30 You can view a page at several different magnifications in the Page Preview dialog.

Previewing Pages in External Browsers

Even though Contribute has its own browser, sometimes you might want to preview a page in a full-fledged Web browser. Contribute allows you to preview pages in the default Web browser for your system. Unlike Dreamweaver, though, Contribute doesn't let you choose multiple browsers to preview.

Previewing a page lets you make sure that the changes you've made look good in a real Web browser, and also allows you to test links before you publish the page. If you're using Dreamweaver templates that contain JavaScript, server-side includes, or image maps for navigation elements such as navigation bars, previewing in an external browser can be a big help.

To preview a page in your browser:

1. Choose File > Preview in Browser, or press F12.

   Contribute displays an alert telling you that it will create a temporary copy of the draft page.

2. Click OK.

   Contribute launches your default browser and displays the page.

✔ Tip

■ You can't view HTML source code in Contribute, so you'll need to use your external browser for that.

Exporting HTML Pages

Normally you'll deal with HTML pages within Contribute, but you also have the option of exporting draft pages as HTML pages that you can save anywhere on your computer or your network. Why might you want to do so? Here's one possible scenario:

You've been working on a draft page that contains important content. The server that you expected to be the page's destination gets taken offline by the IT department. This happens more often than you might think, especially on intranets. Since the server is no longer available, you can't publish the page. But you can export it, allowing you to rescue its content and copy it into a new page, or you can link to it for a site that still works. You can also email the file as an attachment, ensuring that a broken site connection doesn't destroy your hard work.

To export a draft page as HTML:

1. In the Pages panel of the sidebar, select the draft page you want to export.

2. Choose File > Export.
   The Export dialog appears.

3. Navigate to the location where you want to save the file, enter the filename, and click Save.

EDITING
PAGE CONTENT

4

Contribute is all about making it easier to edit the content of Web pages, and the program provides a wide selection of tools to help you create and style your content. Most of these tools will be familiar to you, as they work in ways that are reminiscent of other tools you use, such as word processors. That's no accident: Macromedia made the editing experience as familiar as possible so that users with little or no experience building Web pages could get started quickly with Contribute.

In this chapter, you'll learn how to edit and style text on Web pages, organize your text for easier reading, and check the spelling of your documents before you publish them for all to see.

Basic Text Editing

Like most word-processing and desktop publishing applications, Contribute respects the usual conventions for text entry. You can use the arrow keys, backspace key, Page Up key, Page Down key, and other keys to move around the draft window. As you type, text wraps from line to line. You can cut and paste text, or use drag and drop to move text around. You can also drag text from another application, such as Microsoft Word, into the Contribute draft window.

That's the Breaks

Paragraph breaks in Web-page editors have traditionally used the HTML <p> tag, which Web browsers display by inserting a blank line between paragraphs that use the <p> tag. This is perfectly workable—after all, that's how most Web pages have worked for years—but it doesn't offer the Web-page designer much in the way of typographical control. That control arrived with the advent of Cascading Style Sheets (CSS), an extension to HTML that allows designers to precisely control the formatting and positioning of text. Being a modern Web tool, Contribute understands CSS, and the site administrator can set a user permission that makes Contribute use CSS styles instead of the HTML <p> tag for paragraph breaks. With CSS styles, pressing (Enter) creates a paragraph break without inserting a blank line between paragraphs, so that Contribute works more like a standard word processor (**Figure 4.1**).

> Despite our initially limited broadcast day, it makes sense to build the facility with the broadcast capability to handle our ultimate projected requirements of three full-time channels. It is usually more expensive to add on broadcast capability.
> The facility should be designed to take maximum advantage of automation, so that we can get the most out of our scarce people resources. Better automation will cost more upfront, but will allow us to get the job done with less employee burnout and an operational cost savings.

> Despite our initially limited broadcast day, it makes sense to build the facility with the broadcast capability to handle our ultimate projected requirements of three full-time channels. It is usually more expensive to add on broadcast capability.
>
> The facility should be designed to take maximum advantage of automation, so that we can get the most out of our scarce people resources. Better automation will cost more upfront, but will allow us to get the job done with less employee burnout and an operational cost savings.

Figure 4.1 Paragraph breaks using CSS (top) look more natural than paragraph breaks created with HTML tags (bottom).

Figure 4.2 A paragraph break produces white space above and below the paragraph. Line breaks do not.

To type text into a draft:

1. Browse to the page you want to edit, then click Edit Page to open the page as a draft.

2. Click in the draft window to place the insertion point where you want it, then just start typing your text. If Contribute inserts a blank line when you press [Enter] to make a paragraph break, you can press [Shift]-[Enter] to make a line break that will not include a blank line (**Figure 4.2**).

To copy and paste text into a draft:

1. Select text from a Web page in the browser, another draft page, or another application.

2. Choose Edit > Copy or press [Ctrl]-[C].

3. Click in your Contribute draft to place the insertion point, then choose Edit > Paste, or press [Ctrl]-[V].

✔ Tips

- If you want to paste plain text into Contribute, removing any formatting it had, paste the text by choosing Edit > Paste Text Only, or by pressing [Ctrl]-[Shift]-[V].

- When you have text selected, most of the time you can right-click to cut or copy the text using a shortcut menu. You can also right-click to paste text.

- Contribute offers Undo and Redo commands in the Edit menu, which can often be very useful in fixing mistakes or repeating operations. You can also use the keyboard shortcuts [Ctrl]-[Z] for Undo and [Ctrl]-[Y] for Redo.

BASIC TEXT EDITING

Using HTML Styles

HTML provides quite a few methods for styling and formatting text that allow Web browsers to display text as bold, italic, colored, and so on.

Contribute shields you from the mechanics of HTML; you don't need to know HTML to add formatting to your draft pages. Like word processors, Contribute uses familiar formatting tools, which you can find in the Editing toolbar (**Figure 4.3**) and in the Format and Insert menus.

Setting font styles

The most common text formatting is to make text bold or italicized, change the font, or change the size. Contribute groups controls for these settings together on the Editing toolbar (**Figure 4.4**). Contribute can also format text as Strikethrough (text with a thin line through it), Emphasis (another style of italic text), Strong (another style of bold text), or Fixed Width (text is mono-spaced, like old-fashioned typewriter type, or as in the Courier font).

Your site administrator can allow or deny users the ability to apply HTML styles, so if some of these controls are disabled, you should check with the administrator.

Figure 4.3 The Editing toolbar provides most of the tools you'll need to change the content on your draft pages.

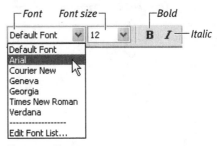

Figure 4.4 The most common text-formatting controls are grouped together on the toolbar.

To make text bold, italic, or underlined:

1. Select the text you want to modify.

2. Click the Bold button on the Editing toolbar, choose Format > Bold, or press [Ctrl]-[B].

   or

   Click the Italic button on the Editing toolbar, Choose Format > Italic, or press [Ctrl]-[I].

   or

   Choose Format > Underline, or press [Ctrl]-[U].

   The text's appearance changes.

✔ Tips

- Though you can underline text with Contribute, I don't recommend it, because people have come to expect that underlined text on Web sites indicates a link.

- To remove a text style, select the text and click the style button again, reselect the menu command, or repeat the shortcut key command. Reapplying the format acts as a toggle, each click turns the formatting on or off.

To format text as Strikethrough, Emphasis, Strong, or Fixed Width:

1. Select the text you want to modify.

2. Choose Format > Other, then pick one of the four choices from the submenu.

✔ Tip

- Your Web administrator may have configured Contribute to use the Strong tag `<strong>` for bold text and the Emphasis tag `<em>` for italic text. These tags tell Contribute to use a more accessible version of the HTML it is creating behind the scenes, helping the visually disabled. You probably won't notice a difference.

Setting fonts and font sizes

In Contribute, you have the ability to set the typeface, or font, for any text on your page. But not all computers or Web browsers use the same fonts. If you specify a font that your site visitor doesn't have on his or her computer, chances are the content won't look the way you intend. Because neither you nor Contribute can be sure what fonts will be available to your site visitors, Contribute uses *font combinations* to work around the problem. Font combinations allow you to provide options for the browser by creating multiple font choices. For example, a font combination could include Arial, Helvetica, and Geneva fonts, and the Web browser would render the page using the first choice available to the browser. If none of the fonts in the combination are installed, the browser will display the text using whatever font is set as the default in the browser's preferences. Contribute comes with six predetermined font combinations, and you can add more as you need them. Each choice in the Font menu represents the first font in that font combination.

Although Contribute is reminiscent of a word processor, it's really not one, and it has the font-size limitations that HTML imposes. In HTML, there are seven standard sizes for fonts, and so it's no surprise that there are also seven size choices in Contribute's Font Size menu. In HTML, these sizes are numbered from 1 to 7; Contribute lists them as their roughly equivalent point sizes, from 8 to 36 (**Figure 4.5**). Contribute doesn't give you the freedom to set custom font sizes, though designers, using CSS styles, can set custom sizes in Macromedia Dreamweaver templates (see the section "Using CSS Styles," in this chapter).

Figure 4.5 The standard HTML font sizes and their Contribute equivalents from the Font Size menu.

The subject of font sizes on Web pages is actually quite complex, and it has generated much gnashing of teeth and heartache between designers, Web-browser makers, and standards bodies. But Contribute makes a valiant attempt—largely successful—to shield you from the furor, so we'll leave the angst to others and get on with building our pages.

To set a font or font size:

1. Select the text you want to modify.

2. Choose a different font from the Font menu in the toolbar, or choose Format > Font, and then choose the font from the submenu.

   or

   Choose a different size from the Font Size menu in the toolbar, or choose Format > Size, and then choose the font size from the submenu.

   The text changes appearance.

✔ Tips

■ Contribute's preset font combinations include fonts that are found on nearly every computer sold in the last several years. Most of these fonts are available for both Windows and Macintosh. For example, Arial, Courier, Georgia, Helvetica, Times New Roman, Verdana, and Trebuchet are all fonts that come standard on both platforms.

■ Contribute doesn't allow you to enter a custom font size, as you can in many word processors.

Changing font combinations

You can modify the preset font combinations, and you can also create new font combinations.

To edit the Font List:

1. In the Pages panel of the sidebar, switch to a new or draft page.

   or

   Browse to a page you want to edit, and then click Edit Page.

2. Choose Format > Font > Edit Font List. The Edit Font List dialog appears (**Figure 4.6**).

3. To add a font combination, click the plus button, then click the arrow buttons in the Available Fonts list and select fonts to move them to the Chosen Fonts list.

   or

   Select a font combination in the Font List, and click the minus button to remove it.

   or

   Use the arrow buttons above the Font List to move a selected font combination up or down in the list.

4. Click OK to save your changes.

✔ Tip

- You can type the name of a font not on your system in the field below the Available Fonts list, then click the left-facing arrow button to add that font to the Chosen Fonts list. You might choose to add a font when you want to use one you know is available on the systems of users who will be visiting your site. For example, if your site will attract many Mac OS X visitors, you can use some of the OS X system fonts, such as Lucida Grande, that are common on the Mac but not on Windows.

Figure 4.6 The Edit Font List dialog lets you define new font combinations.

Figure 4.7 You'll find HTML headings in the Style menu on the toolbar.

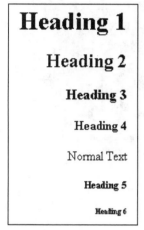

Figure 4.8 Here are examples of the six Heading sizes, plus Normal Text, which is usually used for body text.

Assigning HTML heading styles

HTML supplies six levels of *headings* that you can use to call attention to text on your Web pages. Think of headings as being similar to headlines in a newspaper. They're usually bigger than the body text on the page and are often bold. Headings are what's known as a *paragraph style*, so a line of white space may precede and follow a heading depending on how your Web administrator has set up your site. Heading styles are numbered, with Heading 1 being the largest and Heading 6 the smallest. Headings are selected from Contribute's Style menu on the Editing toolbar (**Figure 4.7**), or by choosing Format > Style. If your Web administrator is using Cascading Style Sheets to format text on your site (see "Using CSS Styles," later in this chapter), these heading choices might not be available.

One other choice appears in the Style menu—Normal, for the style Normal Text, which is the text used for the body of your document (**Figure 4.8**).

To apply a heading style:

1. Click within the line you want to make into a heading to place the insertion point.

2. Select a heading size (1–6) from the Style menu in the Editing toolbar.

   or

   Choose Format > Style, then choose a heading style from the submenu.

   The text is formatted as a heading.

USING HTML STYLES

Coloring and highlighting text

You can select individual blocks of text and change their color, or you can apply a high-lighting effect, in which the background of the text is colored.

To color text:

1. Select the text you want to color.

2. Click the Text Color button in the Editing toolbar (**Figure 4.9**).

   or

   Choose Format > Text Color.

   The color picker appears (**Figure 4.10**).

3. Click a color with the eyedropper to select it; it can be any color in the color picker or any color visible on your desktop or the page you are editing.

   When you select the color, the color picker closes and the text changes color.

To highlight text:

1. Select the text you want to highlight.

2. Click the Highlight Color button in the toolbar.

   or

   Choose Format > Highlight Color.

   The color picker appears.

3. Click a color with the eyedropper to select it; it can be any color in the color picker or any color visible on your desktop or the page you are editing.

   When you select the color, the color picker closes, and the text is highlighted the selected color.

✔ Tip

- Pressing (Esc) closes the color picker without applying a color.

Text Color — —Highlight Color

Figure 4.9 The Text Color and Highlight Color buttons on the Editing toolbar.

Figure 4.10 Use the eyedropper on the color picker to choose your new text color.

Figure 4.11 The text-alignment buttons on the Editing toolbar.

Table 4.1

Alignment Shortcut Keys	
SHORTCUT KEY	WHAT IT DOES
Ctrl-Alt-Shift-L	Left alignment
Ctrl-Alt-Shift-C	Center alignment
Ctrl-Alt-Shift-R	Right alignment
Ctrl-Alt-Shift-J	Full justification

Setting text alignment

Contribute's similarity to a word processor continues with its ability to align text with the left margin, the right margin, or the center of the page. You can also justify text, which adds space as needed between words so that both the left and right margins are aligned.

To align text:

1. Select the text you want to align.

2. On the Editing toolbar, click the Left, Center, Right, or Justify button (**Figure 4.11**).

   or

   Choose Format > Align > and then choose Left, Center, Right, or Justify.

   You can also use the shortcut keys listed in **Table 4.1**.

   The text is aligned according to the option you clicked.

✔ Tip

■ You can change the alignment for a single paragraph, a heading, or an entire page.

Indenting text

You can indent blocks of text in Contribute, but indenting works a little differently here than it does in a word processor. In Word, for example, an indent for a paragraph might pull the left margin of the paragraph in toward the center of the page and might further indent the first line of the paragraph, but would leave the right margin of the paragraph unchanged. The Indent command in Contribute indents the text of the paragraph from both margins (**Figure 4.12**).

To indent text:

1. Click within the paragraph you want to indent, or if you want to indent more than one paragraph, select the text.

2. Click the Indent button on the toolbar (**Figure 4.13**).

   or

   Choose Format > Indent, or press ⌈Ctrl⌉-⌈Alt⌉-⌈]⌉.

   You can increase indent levels by repeating this step.

To remove indents:

1. Click within the paragraph where you want to remove indenting, or if you want to affect more than one paragraph, select the text.

2. Click the Outdent button on the Editing toolbar.

   or

   Choose Format > Outdent, or press ⌈Ctrl⌉-⌈Alt⌉-⌈[⌉.

✔ Tips

- You can often get better control over text placement by using tables rather than indenting. See Chapter 7, "Creating Tables," for more information.

- Contribute does its indenting by applying the HTML <blockquote> tag.

launched by mid-2003, and the Government channel to follow at some future date that would be determined by mutual consultation.

Another possibility that I think that we should explore would be to launch our first channel with combined PEG programming, and plan to split the programming into two or more channels when needed. That would allow us to build interest among all segments of the community from the start, not just the educational crowd.

Figure 4.12 When you indent text, it is indented from both margins.

Outdent ⌐   ⌐ Indent

Figure 4.13 The Indent and Outdent buttons on the toolbar.

Using CSS Styles

From the standpoint of the site designer, the main benefit of using Cascading Style Sheet styles in a Web site is that with CSS, changing the definition of a style changes all the instances that have that style on the site. For example, imagine that a Web designer creates a CSS style named Caution Text that is used on dozens of pages on a site. The text is red, bold, and large (the equivalent of 24 points). After a bit of friendly counseling by his supervisor, the designer tones down Caution Text to be less visually obtrusive. Because the style is a CSS style, changing the definition of Caution Text in the style sheet automatically changes every use of Caution Text in the whole site.

Also from the standpoint of the site designer, by using CSS styles, and by asking the site administrator to disable use of anything other than CSS styles, the designer can make sure that you, the Contribute user, don't have the ability to inadvertently mess up the site design by applying HTML headings, making text bold, or doing things the designer doesn't want. You'll only have the ability to add and edit text and images, which lets the designer sleep at night.

Contribute doesn't let you create CSS styles (you need Dreamweaver or a comparable tool to create style sheets), but you can use the CSS styles that are attached to the site templates. If the designer has created CSS styles, and you have the editing permission to also apply HTML styles, you should use the CSS styles in preference to the HTML styles. It makes your Web site easier to maintain, improves the site's performance for visitors, and makes it easier to change the site in the future, when the inevitable site redesign happens.

continued on next page

As you can see in **Figure 4.14**, the names of CSS styles appear in the Editing toolbar's Style menu along with the seven HTML styles (Normal plus Headings 1 through 6; in Figure 4.14, the site administrator had not disabled HTML styles). The figure also illustrates a drawback of the toolbar's Style menu—that the menu doesn't expand to display the entire name of the CSS style, should the name be longer than the menu is wide. The Style sub-menu of the Format menu shows the entire style name (**Figure 4.15**).

To apply CSS styles:

1. Click within the line you want to style to place the insertion point, or select the text you want to style.

2. Choose Format > Style, then select the CSS style from the Style submenu.

   or

   Choose a CSS style from the Style menu in the Editing toolbar.

Figure 4.14 When a site template includes CSS styles, they appear in the Editing toolbar's Style menu.

Figure 4.15 The Style submenu of the Format menu displays the full names of the CSS styles.

✔ Tips

■ Besides giving finer control over the look of type, CSS styles are useful for positioning elements on the page. Don't be surprised if text moves around as you apply a CSS style to it.

■ You can clear a style and return to the default text style for the page by selecting the text you want to change and then choosing Normal from the Style menu in the Editing toolbar.

■ Some CSS styles are redefined HTML tags. For example, a designer can redefine the Heading 2 style to be a different font as well as bold, centered, and/or in a different text color. You still apply Heading 2 from the Editing toolbar's Style menu, but the effect is different.

■ When you see links on Web pages that are not underlined, or are the same color as the body text but are bold, the trick was done using CSS styles.

■ When you launch Contribute, it connects to each site for which you have a site connection and makes sure that those sites are using the latest versions of the templates on each of them. As part of the same process, Contribute reads the style sheets for the sites.

USING CSS STYLES

Working with Lists

Lists are an easy way to organize content on your Web page. Contribute supports three types of lists:

Numbered lists, for lists with items that need to be in a particular order (**Figure 4.16**). List items are numbered and indented from the left margin. If you add or remove items from the numbered list, it automatically renumbers.

Bulleted lists, for lists of items in no particular order (**Figure 4.17**).

Definition lists, where each item has an indented subitem (**Figure 4.18**).

To create a list:

1. Type the items for your list into the draft window. After typing each item, press [Enter].

2. Select the items in the list.

3. Choose Format > List, then choose Numbered List, Bulleted List, or Definition List from the submenu.

   or

   Click either the Numbered List or Bulleted List button in the Editing toolbar.

✔ Tip

- At the end of your list, you can turn off the list function either by pressing [Enter] twice or by clicking the appropriate list button in the Editing toolbar.

Lucy Kaplansky Discography

1. The Tide (1994)
2. Flesh and Bone (1996)
3. Ten Year Night (1999)
4. Every Single Day (2001)

Lucy Kaplansky Discography

1. The Tide (1994)
2. Flesh and Bone (1996)
3. Cry Cry Cry (1998) w/ Richard Shindell, Dar Williams
4. Ten Year Night (1999)
5. Every Single Day (2001)

Figure 4.16 Numbered lists automatically renumber if you insert a new item between two existing items.

Global Survival Kit

- Metal box
- Survival knife
- Compass
- Fire starter
- Water bag
- Water purification tablets
- Rescue whistle
- Fishing and foraging kit

Figure 4.17 Bulleted lists are single-spaced and indented.

Excerpts from *The Devil's Dictionary*, by Ambrose Bierce
Originally published 1911 (copyright expired)

CHILDHOOD , n.
   The period of human life intermediate between the idiocy of infancy and the folly of youth -- two removes from the sin of manhood and three from the remorse of age.
DAWN , n.
   The time when men of reason go to bed. Certain old men prefer to rise at about that time, taking a cold bath and a long walk with an empty stomach, and otherwise mortifying the flesh.
DELIBERATION , n.
   The act of examining one's bread to determine which side it is buttered on.
NONSENSE , n.
   The objections that are urged against this excellent dictionary.
SCRIBBLER , n.
   A professional writer whose views are antagonistic to one's own.

Figure 4.18 Definition lists have the definitions indented under the definition terms. (The definition terms don't have to be all uppercase—they just happen to be in this figure.)

Figure 4.19 In the List Properties dialog, you can change the way lists are numbered and bulleted.

Table 4.2

List-Numbering Options	
LIST NAME	**EXAMPLE**
Number	1, 2, 3, 4 ...
Roman Small	i, ii, iii, iv ...
Roman Large	I, II, III, IV ...
Alphabet Small	a, b, c, d ...
Alphabet Large	A, B, C, D ...

Setting List Properties

Numbered lists and bulleted lists have properties you can change in Contribute. You can choose between five types of numbering, as shown in **Table 4.2**. For bulleted lists, you can choose either a round bullet (the default) or a square bullet. There are no properties to set for a definition list.

To set list properties:

1. Click in the list you want to change to place the insertion point.

2. Choose Format > List > Properties. The List Properties dialog appears (**Figure 4.19**).

3. Do one or more of the following:

   ▲ In the "List type" pop-up menu, select Bulleted List, Numbered List, or Directory List ("definition list" is called "Directory List" in this dialog for some reason).

   ▲ In the "Style" pop-up menu, select one of the Bulleted List or Numbered List styles.

   ▲ Use the "Start at number" text box to set the value for the first item in the numbered list.

4. Click OK.

✔ Tips

■ If you select an entire numbered or bulleted list, you can't set that list's properties.

■ You cannot set properties for lists within tables, or for lists on pages based on templates.

Nesting lists

You can indent lists within lists to create *nested lists*. Because nested lists do not have to be of the same type, you can create, for example, a numbered list with an indented bulleted list, and you can have multiple levels of nested lists within one overall list (**Figure 4.20**).

To create a nested list:

1. Click the end of a line within an existing list to place the insertion point.

2. Press Enter.

   Another line of the list is created.

3. Press Tab.

   A new indented sublist of the same type as the parent list is created. For example, if the parent list is a numbered list, the new sublist will also be a numbered list.

4. (Optional) If you want the sublist to be a different type of list than the parent list, click the Numbered List or Bulleted List button in the Editing toolbar.

5. Type the list item.

6. Press Enter.

   A new sublist item is created.

7. Press the Enter key twice to leave the sublist.

✔ Tips

■ You can also click the Outdent button in the Editing toolbar to merge the sublist back into the main list.

■ You can use the List Properties dialog to format sublists as well as lists.

1. The Tide (1994)
   - Produced by Shawn Colvin
   - Recorded in New York City
2. Flesh and Bone (1996)

Figure 4.20 You can nest bulleted lists inside numbered lists.

Figure 4.21 Contribute lets you insert dates into your draft pages in a variety of formats.

Inserting Dates

Contribute can insert the current date and time, in a variety of formats, into your Web page. You can choose whether or not to add the day of the week.

To insert the current date:

1. Click in your draft to place the insertion point where you want to date to appear.

2. Choose Insert > Date.

   The Insert Date dialog appears (**Figure 4.21**).

3. Do one or more of the following:

   ▲ If you want the day to appear, use the "Day format" pop-up menu to set the appearance of the day of the week.

   ▲ Make a selection from the "Date format" list.

   ▲ If you want the time to appear, choose the 12-hour or 24-hour format from the "Time format" list.

   ▲ Select the "Update automatically on save" check box, if you want that to happen. This is very useful if you want visitors to your site to know when the page was last updated.

4. Click OK.

   Contribute inserts the date (and possibly the time) into your draft page.

Adding Horizontal Rules

A *horizontal rule* is a line that runs across the page, providing a division between parts of the document (**Figure 4.22**). By default, a horizontal rule in Contribute is the width of the page, is 1 pixel high, and has a small drop shadow. You can change these properties if you want.

To insert a horizontal rule:

1. Click in the page to place the insertion point where you want the horizontal rule to appear.

2. Choose Insert > Horizontal Rule.

A line appears as wide as the page.

To modify a horizontal rule's properties:

1. Click the horizontal rule to select it.

2. Right-click the horizontal rule, and then choose Properties from the shortcut menu.

The Horizontal Rule Properties dialog appears (**Figure 4.23**).

3. Do one or more of the following:

▲ Type a number in the Width field, and choose either "pixels" or "percent" from the pop-up menu. Choosing "pixels" creates a fixed-width line; choosing "percent" creates a line that expands or contracts depending on the width of the site visitor's browser window.

▲ In the Height text box, type a number for the horizontal rule. This height is measured in pixels.

▲ If you select the Use Outline Shading check box, the line appears as an outline rather than as a solid line.

4. Click OK.

Figure 4.22 This horizontal rule separates two sections of the draft page.

Figure 4.23 You can change the width and height of a horizontal rule in the Horizontal Rule Properties dialog.

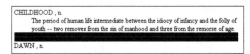

Figure 4.24 When you select the rule, you can see the white space above and below it.

✔ Tips

■ The horizontal rule has white space above and below it, which you can see if you click the rule to select it (**Figure 4.24**).

■ Horizontal rules are a leftover from the early days of HTML. Use them sparingly, if at all, because they tend to make a page look dated.

Non-Breaking Space	Ctrl+Shift+Space
Copyright	
Registered Trademark	
Trademark	
Pound	
Yen	
Euro	
Left Quote	
Right Quote	
Em Dash	
Other...	

Figure 4.25 The most common special characters are available from the Insert > Special Characters submenu.

Figure 4.26 The Insert Other Character dialog provides the rest of the special characters Contribute can insert.

Inserting Special Characters

You can add special characters, such as the Euro, copyright, or trademark symbols, to your page in Contribute without having to remember their bizarre HTML equivalents. Relief is just a menu choice away.

To insert a special character:

1. Click in the page to place the insertion point where you want the special character to appear.

2. Choose Insert > Special Characters, then choose the special character you want from the submenu (**Figure 4.25**).

   or

   If the character you want doesn't appear in the menu, choose Other. The Insert Other Character dialog appears (**Figure 4.26**).

3. Click the character you want to use, then click OK to close the dialog.

   The special character is placed on your page.

Finding and Replacing Text

Contribute has a fairly rudimentary Find and Replace feature that can search the current draft document for a particular piece of text and then replace that text with another.

To find text:

1. With the draft page you want to search displayed, choose Edit > Find, or press Ctrl-F.

   The Find and Replace dialog appears (**Figure 4.27**).

2. In the "Search for" text box, type the text you're looking for.

3. (Optional) If you want to match the case pattern (uppercase or lowercase) of the text you type in the "Search for" text box, select the "Match case" check box.

4. Click Find Next.

   Contribute searches the draft, and if the text is found, it highlights the text in the document window. If Contribute does not find the text, a dialog appears telling you so.

5. If you want to continue searching, click Find Next again. Otherwise, click Close.

Figure 4.27 Contribute can find and replace text on your draft page.

To find and replace text:

1. With the draft page you want to search displayed, choose Edit > Find, or press `Ctrl`-`F`.

   The Find and Replace dialog appears.

2. In the "Search for" field, type the text you're looking for.

3. (Optional) If you want to match the case pattern (uppercase or lowercase) of the text you type in the "Search for" text box, select the "Match case" check box.

4. Type the text you want as the replacement in the "Replace with" text box.

5. Click Find Next. Contribute finds the first instance of the search text.

6. Click Replace.

7. (Optional) If you want to have Contribute automatically replace all the found text with the contents of the "Replace with" text box, click Replace All.

   Contribute displays a dialog telling you how many replacements were made.

8. Click Close to return to the draft window.

Checking Spelling

No word processor comes without a spelling checker these days, and neither does Contribute. You can check the spelling on a draft page and add words to Contribute's spelling checker in a personal dictionary.

To spell-check your draft:

1. With the draft page you want to spell-check displayed, click the Check Spelling button on the Editing toolbar (**Figure 4.28**), or choose Format > Check Spelling or press F7.

   If Contribute finds a word it believes is spelled incorrectly, the Check Spelling dialog appears (**Figure 4.29**).

2. Click Add to Personal if the word Contribute found is correct and you want to add it to your personal dictionary so that Contribute doesn't flag it as an error again.

   or

   Click Ignore to tell the spelling checker to ignore this instance of the word, or Ignore All to ignore the word throughout the document.

   or

   Select a replacement from the "Suggestions" list, or type the replacement in the "Change to" text box. Then click the Change button, or click Change All to replace the word throughout the document.

3. When the spelling check is finished, click Close.

✔ Tip

■ Even if you place the insertion point in the draft page, the spelling checker always starts at the top of the page.

Figure 4.28 Trigger the spelling checker with the Check Spelling button on the Editing toolbar.

Figure 4.29 Click Add to Personal in the Check Spelling dialog to add an unknown word (such as your last name) to Contribute's personal dictionary.

Working with Images

Images and media files convey an important amount of the information on your Web site. Although you'll probably get most of your message across with text (I guess it's not surprising that a writer would say that), graphics can provide a great deal of visual interest, and attractive graphics go a long way toward bringing visitors back to your site.

On the other hand, we've all seen Web sites that suffer from graphic overkill. It's always a bad sign when your site's visitors clutch their faces and scream, "My eyes! My eyes! *Aieeee!*" So while Macromedia Contribute makes it easy to add images and media files to your Web pages, don't forget that less is often more when it comes to Web design.

Adding Images to Your Pages

If an image is accessible to you either locally or on one of your Web sites, Contribute can place it in your draft Web pages. You can insert images from your hard drive or local network, from other applications, reuse an image from elsewhere on your Web site, or use an image from another Contribute draft page. There are slightly different techniques for inserting images from your computer or inserting images from your Web site.

To insert images from your computer:

1. Begin editing the page where you want to place the image. For more information on how to begin editing pages, see Chapter 3, "Building Web Pages."

   If the page you're editing is based on a template, the template will most likely have a place for the image to go, and perhaps even a placeholder image (**Figure 5.1**). If the page contains a placeholder image that you want to replace with the new image, you should first delete the placeholder image by clicking it and pressing Bksp, or by choosing Edit > Clear.

2. Place the insertion point where you want the image to appear, and then choose Insert > Image > From My Computer, or press Ctrl-Alt-I. The Select Image dialog appears (**Figure 5.2**).

3. Navigate to the image file you want to insert, select it in the Select Image dialog, and click the Select button.

   The image appears on your draft Web page (**Figure 5.3**).

Placeholder image ⌐

Navigation bar (noneditable) ⌐

Editable template area

Figure 5.1 This is a new page, based on a Dreamweaver template, that is being edited in Contribute. Note that only part of the page can be edited and that the image on the page is only there as a placeholder.

Figure 5.2 In the Select Image dialog, choose the image you want to place on the page.

Figure 5.3 The new image goes where the placeholder image was.

Figure 5.4 The Choose Image on Website dialog allows you to browse the files on your Web sites, rather than on your computer.

Figure 5.5 The Preview section of the dialog makes it easier to find the image you want.

To insert images from your Web site:

1. Begin editing the page where you want to place the image.

2. Place the insertion point where you want the image to appear, and then choose Insert > Image > From Website.

   The Choose Image on Website dialog appears (**Figure 5.4**). Rather than browsing through the folder structure on your hard drive, this dialog browses the folder structure from the Web sites you have defined as Connections in Contribute. Each of the defined sites will appear in the dialog.

3. Double-click the Web site that contains the image you want, then find and select the image file.

   Contribute shows you a preview of the image you are browsing (**Figure 5.5**).

4. Click OK to insert the image into your Web page.

continued on next page

✔ Tips

- You can also add images to your Web pages by dragging and dropping them from some Windows applications directly into the draft Web page in Contribute. Not all applications work (unfortunately, you can't drag and drop from Macromedia's own Fireworks), but you can drag images from any of the Microsoft Office applications, Internet Explorer, Windows Explorer, or directly from your desktop. If you're not sure if drag and drop works from a particular program into Contribute, just try it. You might need to resize the windows of either Contribute or the other application in order to see both images onscreen at the same time.

- Another handy way to add a graphic to pages in Contribute is to copy the image from another application (such as Microsoft Internet Explorer), then paste it into your draft Web page.

- Normally, when you place an image file on a draft Web page that resides on your local hard drive or your network, Contribute uploads a copy of the image to the server when you publish the page. But what if the image is already on your server (because you used the image on another page)? Contribute will recognize that the file is already part of your Web site and will not upload another copy of the image file.

- The site administrator can specify that Contribute always prompt you to enter *alternative* descriptive text (sometimes known as the ALT tag) whenever you insert an image. This alternative text is used when the Web browser viewing the page has disabled viewing images, or used with alternative Web browsers designed for people with visual disabilities.

ADDING IMAGES TO YOUR PAGES

Image Types

To be used in Contribute, an image must already be in one of the three Web-ready graphic formats:

- ◆ JPEG

- ◆ GIF

- ◆ PNG

If the image is in another graphic format, such as BMP or TIF, you must convert it to one of the Web-ready formats before attempting to place it in Contribute. To do the conversion, you'll need an image-editing program, such as Macromedia Fireworks or Microsoft Paint.

To delete images:

1. In your draft Web page, select the image you want to delete.

2. Press `Bksp`, or choose Edit > Clear.

✔ Tip

■ If you accidentally delete an image, you can get it back by choosing Edit > Undo Image or by pressing `Ctrl`-`Z`. Remember that Contribute can, by default, undo the last 50 actions, and you can increase the number of undo steps in the General category of Contribute's Preferences (Edit > Preferences).

Where Do the Images Go?

When you add images to Contribute pages, Contribute automatically creates a subdirectory of the current directory (the one that contains the page that references the new image) called *images*, and uploads the images for that page to the *images* directory. Images for any other pages in the current directory are also placed in the *images* subdirectory.

If you already have an *images* directory inside the current directory on the server, the new image is copied to that *images* directory. This is all done automatically for you. Unfortunately, Contribute doesn't allow you to specify where new images are to be placed on the server, so you can't have a single, separate *images* directory on the same level as your *pages* directory.

Adjusting Image Properties

Once you have added an image to a page, you can modify the image's properties. You can change the image; change the image's size; change the image's alignment and border; and change the image's descriptive, or alternative, text (ALT text).

To modify image properties:

1. While editing a draft page, double-click the image you want to modify.

   or

   Choose Format > Image Properties.

   or

   Right-click the image, then choose Image Properties from the shortcut menu.

   Regardless of the method used, the Image Properties dialog appears (**Figure 5.6**).

2. Make the changes you want. See **Table 5.1** for details about each of the controls in the Image Properties dialog.

3. Click OK.

Figure 5.6 You can change many of an image's attributes in the Image Properties dialog.

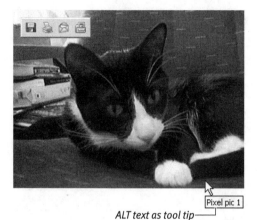

ALT text as tool tip ———

Figure 5.7 ALT text appears as a pop-up tool tip in many Web browsers.

✔ Tips

- You can add a border around an image with the Image Properties dialog, but there's no way to change the border's color from Contribute's default color of black.

- It's a good idea to add ALT text to all of your images. Not only will it make your pages more accessible for the disabled, but it might also be easier for your pages to be read by people who are using small-screen devices, such as mobile phones. Many browsers also show the ALT text displayed as a tool tip when the user mouses over the image (**Figure 5.7**).

Table 5.1

Image Properties Dialog

PROPERTY OR CONTROL	WHAT IT DOES
Image file	Shows the path to the image file. The Browse button next to this field is a pop-up menu that allows you to find and select image files on your Web sites, or files on your computer.
Width	Sets the width of the image file. You can choose the width either in pixels or as a percentage of the current image size from the pop-up menu next to this field.
Height	Sets the height of the image file. You can choose the height either in pixels or as a percentage of the current image size from the pop-up menu next to this field.
Reset Size	Returns the image to its original size if you have made changes.
Constrain proportions	Makes sure that changes to width or height are proportional. For example, if you increase the image's width by 50%, the image's height will also increase by 50%.
Horizontal padding	Sets the amount of horizontal blank space to the left and right of the image, in pixels.
Vertical padding	Sets the amount of vertical blank space at the top and bottom of the image, in pixels.
Alignment	Sets the location of the image on the page in relation to text around the image. The pop-up menu choices are Default, which aligns the bottom of the image with the baseline of the text or the nearest object; Left; Right; Middle, which aligns the middle of the image with the text baseline; or Top, which aligns the image's top with the top of the nearest object on the page. The graphic to the right of the pop-up menu changes to show you the effects of each choice.
Border	Sets the width of the border around the image, in pixels.
Description (ALT text)	Allows you to enter text that describes the image for browsers with images turned off, or for people with visual disabilities who use text-to-speech browsers.

Resizing images

You resize images in Contribute by dragging the image's selection handles, or if you want more precise control, by specifying a height or width in the Image Properties dialog.

To resize an image:

1. Select the image.

2. Click one of the image's selection handles, and drag the handle until the image is the desired size (**Figure 5.8**).

   Holding down Shift while you drag the handle constrains the proportions of the image so that it isn't distorted as you resize it.

   or

   Double-click the image, then change its height or width in the Image Properties dialog that appears (**Figure 5.6**). You can specify height and width values either as dimensions measured in pixels or as a percentage of the image size.

   Click the "Constrain proportions" check box to prevent the image from being distorted.

✔ Tip

- Contribute's ability to resize images smoothly is limited. You will often get better results using an actual image-editing application, such as Macromedia Fireworks or Adobe Photoshop, to resize images *before* you use them in Contribute.

Figure 5.8 When you drag an image's selection handle to resize the image, the dotted line shows you what the new size of the image will be when you release the mouse button.

Figure 5.9 Use Contribute's File Editors preferences to select an external editor for a given image type.

Editing Images

Contribute doesn't allow you to edit images directly, other than resizing them. Instead, it hands off the editing task to another program on your computer, such as Fireworks, which is selected by default. If you want to specify another program for image editing, such as Adobe Photoshop, you can do so in the File Editors category of Contribute's Preferences (**Figure 5.9**). Choose Edit > Preferences, select the File Editors category, then make your selection.

When you tell Contribute to edit an image file that has already been placed on one of your Web pages, Contribute uses the external editing program to edit the copy of the file on your Web server. If the file also exists as the original source file on your hard drive, it will not be edited, and changes to the original source file will not be automatically reflected in Contribute. Here's an example. If you build a Web page that contains the image file `kitten.jpg`, when you publish the page, Contribute makes a copy of the `kitten.jpg` file and uploads that copy to the server. If you then go back and edit the page using Contribute and edit the `kitten.jpg` file, the file that is edited will be the copy of `kitten.jpg` on the server.

✔ Tip

- When setting File Editors preferences, you can add image types to the list by clicking the plus button above the Extensions list. For each image type, you can also choose multiple external editors by clicking the plus button above the Editors column. When you select an editor from the list, and click the Make Primary button, Contribute will make that external editor the preferred editor for the selected image type.

To edit an image

1. In Contribute's Edit mode, right-click the image you want to edit, and choose Edit Image from the shortcut menu (**Figure 5.10**).

Contribute creates a new draft page that contains only the image, then displays a window titled Editing Draft in Another Application (**Figure 5.11**), and launches the external editing program specified in Contribute's Preferences.

If you're using Macromedia Fireworks as the editing application, Fireworks displays the Find Source dialog, asking if you want to edit a source file for the image (**Figure 5.12**). Click No.

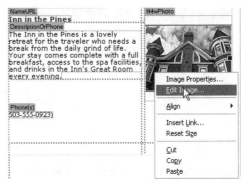

Figure 5.10 Begin editing an image by right-clicking it and choosing Edit Image from the shortcut menu.

Figure 5.11 After the Edit button is clicked, Contribute launches the external image editor and displays this informational window.

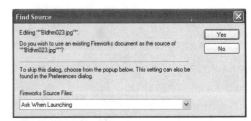

Figure 5.12 If you're using Fireworks as your image editor, it asks if you want to edit the source file rather than Contribute's copy on the server.

Figure 5.13 In Fireworks' editing window, click the Done button to save the file and return to Contribute.

Figure 5.14 Use Contribute's Pages panel to return to the draft page you are editing.

2. Make your changes to the image in the external editing application. If you're using Fireworks, click the Done button in the editing window when you're finished (**Figure 5.13**). If you're using another program, save and close the file when you are finished editing.

3. Switch back to Contribute.

4. Click Publish in the toolbar to save the edited image to the Web site.

Contribute returns to Browse mode and displays the page that contains only the now-changed image.

5. To continue editing the draft of the original page that contains the changed image, click its name in Contribute's Pages panel (**Figure 5.14**).

Replacing images

In the preceding scenario, you're making changes to a copy of the original source file on your Web site. But what if you make changes to the actual source file, and then want to replace the copy of the file on the Web server with a new copy of the changed source file? You cannot simply edit the page that the image file is on and replace the image, because Contribute will not overwrite files with the same name. As a safety measure, Contribute has a feature called *filename collision* that automatically renames a file if that file has the same name as a file already on the server. In this case, however, Contribute is being a little too clever; you want to overwrite files, because you probably don't want several versions of a file sitting on your Web server. Instead, you'll have to manually delete the old version of the file and replace it with the new version.

Understanding Contribute's Filename Collision

Because Contribute is designed to be extremely easy to use, even for people who have never edited Web pages before, it attempts to shield you from many of the details of working with files on your Web site. One of the things the program does is to automatically rename files that have identical filenames already on the server. This renaming process avoids filename collision without asking the user to choose another filename when the draft page is published. Contribute does this by adding numbers to the end of the filename. For example, if you already have a file named `incrediblepicture.jpg` on your site, and you attempt to add another image with the same name, Contribute automatically (and without letting you know) renames the new version `incrediblepicture_000.jpg` when you click the Publish button.

As pages are repeatedly edited, it's possible to end up with several differently named copies of nearly identical files, only one of which is actually being used on a page. Using Dreamweaver, the site's administrator can delete unwanted duplicate files.

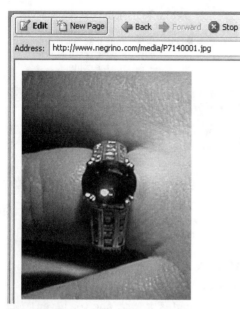

Figure 5.15 Browse to the image you want to replace so that it appears alone.

To replace an image with another image of the same name:

1. Use Contribute's browser to browse directly to the image file, so that it appears by itself in the Contribute window (**Figure 5.15**).

2. Choose File > Delete Page.

   If Delete Page is disabled, it is because your site's administrator has not enabled you to delete editable files. Contact your site administrator, or if you are the site administrator, see "Assigning permissions" in Chapter 10 for more information.

3. Browse to a page that used the now-deleted image.

   The page displays a broken image icon where the image was.

4. Click Edit on the toolbar.

5. Choose Insert > Image > From My Computer (or Insert > Image > From Website).

   The appropriate image selection dialog appears.

6. Navigate to the new version of the image, select it in the dialog, and then click Select.

   The new image appears on your draft page.

7. Click the Publish button in the toolbar to save the new image to the server.

✔ Tip

■ If the image you are replacing appears on other pages on your site, it is very important that the image have exactly the same name and be located in exactly the same place on the Web server as the image you are replacing. This can be tricky to accomplish with Contribute. Usually, you should use a more powerful product like Dreamweaver to make any changes that affect multiple pages on your Web site.

Adding Flash Content

You can add Macromedia Flash movies to your Contribute pages as easily as you add any other image. When you insert a Flash file into a page, Contribute uploads a copy of the file to the server when you publish the page, just as it does with image files.

To insert a Flash file:

1. In Edit mode, put the insertion point where you want the Flash movie to appear.

2. Choose Insert > Flash Movie.

   The Select File dialog appears.

3. Navigate to the Flash file you want, select it, then click the Select button.

   The Flash movie appears in your document. It may be represented by a place-holder with the Flash icon (**Figure 5.16**).

When used with some Web sites, Contribute doesn't show the content of the Flash file while you're editing the page. When this occurs, you must publish the page and view it in Contribute's browser (or Internet Explorer) to see the full effect of the Flash movie on your page.

To change a Flash file's properties:

1. In editing mode, double-click the Flash movie.

   The Flash Movie Properties dialog opens (**Figure 5.17**).

2. Choose one or both of the two options (both are selected by default).

3. Click OK.

Figure 5.16 In Edit mode, some Flash movies may appear as placeholders; in which case you can't see the content.

Figure 5.17 You can control only two of the Flash movie's parameters.

✔ Tips

- If you attempt to view a Flash movie in Contribute's browser and you haven't previously installed the free Macromedia Flash Player plug-in, you'll be prompted to install it. Installing the player will also make the Flash Player available when you use Internet Explorer.

- If Contribute crashes when editing Web pages containing Flash movies, update to the latest version of the Macromedia Flash Player MX, available from the Macromedia Web site (www.macromedia.com/downloads/).

- Contribute does not have an easy way to add media files other than Flash animations to your pages. You can add links to your pages that point to media files, such as MP3, WAV, Windows Media, or QuickTime files, and Contribute will upload those files to your server, but you won't be able to control their properties, preview, or play them in Contribute. If you need to use other kinds of media files in your pages, you should use a full-featured Web creation program, such as Dreamweaver MX.

- The name of the Flash file appears in the Flash Movie Properties dialog.

WORKING WITH LINKS

Hyperlinks, or more commonly just called *links*, are the lifeblood of Web pages, and Macromedia Contribute gives you a rich set of tools you can use to link to other Web pages on your site, Web addresses of pages on other sites, email addresses, non-HTML files on your Web server, and more. Contribute can create links from text or graphics on the pages you are editing to any of the above destinations.

Links consist of two parts: the text or image that the user of your Web page sees and clicks, sometimes called the *hot spot*; and the *URL*, or Uniform Resource Locator, which is the address that tells the browser where to go to follow the link.

In this chapter, you'll learn how to use Contribute to handle all of your hyperlinking needs, by creating and editing links that will connect your Web pages to other pages on your site, or to the rest of the world.

About Linking

Contribute can create hyperlinks to any content it can browse to, whether the content is a file on your computer, a page that's been published on your Web site, a page that's still in draft form, or documents elsewhere on the Web. Note that what you link to doesn't necessarily have to be a Web page; the link can go to a downloadable file, a media clip such as a movie or Flash animation, or an image.

You'll use two kinds of links in Contribute:

◆ **Absolute links**, which include the entire URL to the page, such as http://www.negrino.com/pages/books.html Absolute links usually point to a page that's not on the site where the current page is located. When you create a link in Contribute to a page that's outside of the current site, Contribute always uses an absolute link.

◆ **Relative links** include just a part of the URL and point to a document within the current site. In the example above, a relative link to the page from another page on the same site would be books.html. Contribute automatically creates relative links when you link to a page within the current site.

The good news about using Contribute to create links is that you don't have to worry about the kind of link you're using, because Contribute automatically creates the kind of link that's best in a particular situation.

✔ Tip

■ To control the colors of links on your pages, while you're editing a page, choose Format > Page Properties, or press [Ctrl]-[J]. In the Page Properties dialog box you can specify the link color, the visited-link color, and the active-link color. If these options are not available in Page Properties, it's probably because you're editing a page based on a template or you've been restricted to text-only page editing by your administrator. For more information, see "Setting Page Properties" in Chapter 3.

Figure 6.1 The Insert Link dialog allows you to link to draft pages you've created in Contribute but haven't yet published.

Linking to Draft Pages

Contribute makes links to pages that are in the editing process differently from the way it makes links to pages that have already been created and published. If you think about it for a moment, this makes perfect sense; you can't use Contribute's built-in browser to browse to and edit pages that Contribute hasn't yet published, because they don't have a Web address to browse to yet. So Contribute gives you a way to link to the pages it knows about, even though they've yet to "officially" appear on your site. Of course, you can also use Contribute to make links to pages that are already live on your site; see "Linking to Web Addresses," later in this chapter.

In terms of linking, Contribute treats a new page on your site that is not yet saved or published the same as if it were a draft page.

To create a link to a new or draft page on your site:

1. Select the text or image you want to make into a link.

2. Choose Insert > Link > Drafts and Recent Pages, or press Ctrl-Alt-L.

   or

   In the toolbar, click the Link pop-up menu, and choose Drafts and Recent Pages.

   or

   Right-click the selected text or image, and choose Insert Link from the shortcut menu.

   The Insert Link dialog appears, with the Drafts and Recent Pages button already selected (**Figure 6.1**).

continued on next page

3. The selected text appears in the "Link text" field of the dialog (if you're linking to an image, the "Link text" field doesn't appear). The new or draft pages that are available to you appear in the list below. Select one of the pages in the list.

A thumbnail of the page appears in the Preview section of the dialog.

4. (Optional) Click the Advanced button to expand the Insert Link dialog (**Figure 6.2**).

5. (Optional) You can change the address of the page that's being linked to by modifying the contents of the HREF field. If the page to which you want to point the link has section anchors, they will appear in the "Section anchor" pop-up menu, and you can select the anchor there. You can find more information about section anchors in the "Adding and Editing Anchors" section of this chapter. If you want the link to create a new window when clicked, choose New Window from the "Target frame" pop-up menu.

6. Click OK to create the link to the selected page.

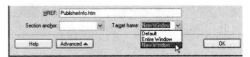

Figure 6.2 The Advanced section of the Insert Link dialog lets you target the destination of your link.

✔ Tips

- Contribute automatically fills in the HREF field in the Advanced section of the Insert Link dialog when you select the draft page for the link, basing the HREF on the name of that page. If you change the contents of the HREF field, you'll change the link destination, and you won't link to the page you selected. The main benefit of the HREF field is to tell you the actual name of the page as that file will appear on the Web server; the name of the page in Figure 6.2 is the page title.

- When you click the Advanced button, Contribute scans the selected page for section anchors, which appear in the "Section anchor" pop-up menu. If the page contains no anchors, you'll see <No anchors found> in the pop-up menu.

Setting Page Targets

In the "Target frame" pop-up menu in the Advanced portion of the Insert Link dialog, you can choose which browser frame, or *target*, displays as the result of clicking the link. If the page you're linking to contains named frames, you'll see the frame names in the pop-up menu. Besides these named frames, you'll have three choices (which also appear when the page you're linking to has no named frames). Many Contribute users will be familiar with Dreamweaver, yet the two programs use different terminology for the same actions (Contribute tries to be more user-friendly and less code-oriented). I've included the Dreamweaver equivalent for the three target choices. Not surprisingly, the Dreamweaver equivalent is also the entry that would need to be in the target= portion of the Anchor HTML tag—the tag that creates links.

- **Default** opens the new page in the same frame as the current page. The Dreamweaver equivalent is _self.

- **Entire window** replaces the frameset with the linked page. The Dreamweaver equivalent target is _top.

- **New window** loads the linked page in a new browser window. Dreamweaver's equivalent target is _blank. Use this choice when the page you're linking to doesn't have frames; it allows you to easily open new windows with links.

Creating New Pages from Links

When you're adding to a site, you'll often want to create a link to a new page on the site. Contribute allows you to make the link and create the new page in one operation. Although you can create new pages on your site using Contribute's New Page command, it's easier to create pages and links simultaneously than it is to create pages and then link them later.

To create a new page from a link:

1. Select the text or image you want to make into a link.

2. Choose Insert > Link > Create New Page.

   or

   In the toolbar, click the Link pop-up menu and choose Create New Page.

   or

   Right-click the selected text or image, and choose Insert Link from the shortcut menu.

   The Insert Link dialog appears. If you used the menu bar or the toolbar to bring up this dialog, the Create New Page button will already be selected (**Figure 6.3**). If you used the shortcut menu, you'll need to click the Create New Page button in the dialog.

Figure 6.3 In the Insert Link dialog, you can create a blank new page, or you can base the new page on Sample Pages or Templates.

Figure 6.4 The Sample Web Pages folder contains a variety of generic but serviceable canned pages you can use as a jumping-off point for your own modifications.

Figure 6.5 Templates are custom pages created in Dreamweaver that you can use to create new pages in Contribute.

3. By default, the Blank Web Page choice will be selected. If you want to create a new blank page in your site, go to step 4.

   ▲ If you want the new page to be based on one of the Sample Pages, click the plus button next to the Sample Web Pages folder to disclose its contents, then choose the page you want (**Figure 6.4**).

   ▲ If you want the new page to be based on one of the Templates, click the plus button next to the Templates folder to disclose its contents, then choose the template you want to use (**Figure 6.5**). These templates are designated by the site administrator.

4. In the "New page title" field, enter the title of the page as you want it to appear in a Web browser.

5. (Optional) If you want the new page to open in a new browser window when the user clicks the link, click the Advanced button in the Insert Link dialog, and choose New Window from the "Target frame" pop-up menu.

6. Click OK to create the link and the new page. Contribute creates and displays the new draft page, ready for you to edit and publish.

✔ Tips

- If Sample Pages or Templates is missing from the Insert Link dialog, it might be because your site administrator has disabled these features for you. Check with your site administrator if you're unsure. See Chapter 10, "Site Administration," for more information about administering Contribute sites.

- If you selected an image for your link, the "Link text" field will not appear in the Insert Link dialog.

CREATING NEW PAGES FROM LINKS

Linking to Web Addresses

When you want to link to other Web pages, either ones that are already published on your site or elsewhere on the Web, you use the Browse to Web Page option from Contribute's Insert Link dialog.

It's helpful if you know the URL of the page you want to link to, but if you don't, no worries—you can use Contribute's built-in browser to find the page you want.

To link to a Web address:

1. Select the text or image you want to make into a link.

2. Choose Insert > Link > Browse to Web Page, or choose Browse to Web Page from the Link pop-up menu in the toolbar. The Insert Link dialog opens (**Figure 6.6**).

3. Enter the URL of the page you want to link to in the "Web address (URL)" field.

   or

   If you don't know the URL, click the Browse button. The Browse to Link dialog appears. This dialog is actually a Web browser and works like any other browser window; use it to browse to the page you want to link to (**Figure 6.7**). When the page you want is displayed, click OK.

4. The target page for the link is now displayed in the Preview box of the Insert Link dialog. Click OK to create the link.

Figure 6.6 You can link to Web pages external to your site by browsing to the destination Web page.

Figure 6.7 The Browse to Link dialog is actually a miniature Web browser.

✔ Tips

■ The Browse to Link window is resizable; you can adjust its size as you would any other window, by dragging an edge of the window.

■ You don't have to link just to other Web pages. You can link to any content with a URL, including file downloads via FTP; media files such as Flash, QuickTime, or Windows Media movies; or anything else. Just enter the URL of the item you want to link to in the "Web address (URL)" field.

■ Don't forget that you can copy URLs from your standalone Web browser, such as Internet Explorer, and paste them into the "Web address (URL)" field. This is often faster than browsing to the target page.

■ If necessary, you can edit the URL in either the "Web address (URL)" field or the HREF field that's displayed when you click the Advanced button at the bottom of the Insert Link dialog.

LINKING TO WEB ADDRESSES

Creating Email Links

When a link to an email address on a Web page is clicked, the Web browser passes the request to an email program, which creates a new outgoing message with that address. Once again, use the Insert Link dialog to create an email address link.

To create an email link:

1. Select the text or image you want to make into a link.

2. Choose Insert > Link > E-mail Address, or choose E-mail Address from the Link pop-up menu in the toolbar.

    The Insert Link dialog opens, with the selected text already inserted in the "Link text" field (**Figure 6.8**).

3. In the "E-mail address" field, type in the address. Click OK.

✔ Tip

■ Clicking the Advanced button in the Insert Link dialog shows you the full email address link in its HTML form—that is, `mailto:me@myaddress.com`. Because `mailto` links open email programs, not other Web pages, the "Section anchor" and "Target frame" pop-up menus are disabled.

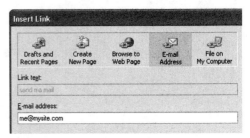

Figure 6.8 Enter the destination email address in order to create an email link.

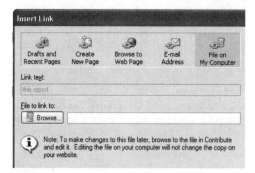

Figure 6.9 You can link to files on your computer when you choose File on My Computer.

Figure 6.10 Use the Select File dialog to navigate to the file you want to upload to your Web site.

Linking to Local Files

Contribute lets you link to a document that resides on your local hard drive or to documents that reside on network disks that are connected to your computer. For example, you can make a link to a local text or image file, a Word file, or a PDF document. When you publish the page that contains the link, Contribute uploads a copy of the document to your Web site, where it resides in the same directory as the HTML pages on your site. When users click the link on your Web site, their browser downloads a copy of the file.

You use this linking method to create links to items you want users of your Web site to be able to download.

To link to files on your computer or network:

1. Select the text or image you want to make into a link.

2. Choose Insert > Link > File on My Computer, or choose File on My Computer from the Link pop-up menu in the toolbar.

   The Insert Link dialog opens, with the selected text already inserted in the "Link text" field (**Figure 6.9**).

3. Click the Browse button.

   The Select File dialog appears (**Figure 6.10**).

continued on next page

LINKING TO LOCAL FILES

4. Navigate to the file you want to upload and link to, select the file, and click the Select button.

If the file resides on a network volume, Contribute may ask you to save a copy of the file on your local hard drive. If the File Download or Save As dialog appears, click Save and save a copy of the file on your hard drive.

5. Click OK to close the Insert Link dialog.

6. Contribute displays a dialog that reminds you that it will make a copy of the file on your Web site, and that in order to edit the file, you need to edit the copy on your Web site, not the one on your computer (**Figure 6.11**). Click OK.

When you publish the page, Contribute uploads a copy of the file to your Web site.

✔ Tip

■ If the name of the file you're uploading contains any special characters, including ampersand, comma, slash, hyphen, asterisk, number sign, or some others, Contribute will display an alert dialog letting you know that some Web servers won't access the files properly. You should rename the file to eliminate these characters before you upload the file.

Figure 6.11 Once you've uploaded the file, Contribute reminds you that you'll need to edit the copy on your Web site, not the one on your computer.

LINKING TO LOCAL FILES

Figure 6.12 Enter the section anchor name.

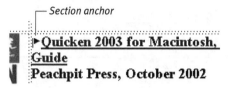

Figure 6.13 The section anchor's icon only appears in Contribute's Edit mode.

Adding and Editing Anchors

A *section anchor* (sometimes called a *named anchor*) is a link to a specific location on a Web page. Whereas regular links point to an entire document, section anchors link to a place in the document. You use section anchors when you want to direct visitors to a specific place within a page, rather than to the top of the page.

There are two parts to working with anchors. First, you need to name the part of the page where you want to link, which creates the anchor. Then you need to link to the anchor from another page.

To add a section anchor:

1. On the page where you want the anchor, click to put the insertion point at the anchor point, or select the text or image to which you want the anchor to be attached. This will be the destination of the anchor.

2. Choose Insert > Section Anchor, or press Ctrl-Alt-A.
   The Section Anchor dialog appears.

3. Enter the name you want for the section anchor (**Figure 6.12**).

   I suggest that you use a single lowercase word or number for the name, with no spaces.

4. Click OK.

   A small flag icon appears at the anchor point on the Web page. (**Figure 6.13**). This icon only shows when you are in Edit mode in Contribute. The flag icon does not appear when you're in Contribute's Browse mode, or when visitors are viewing the page on the Web.

✔ Tip

■ If you can't see the section anchor flag icons in editing mode, you might need to adjust one of Contribute's Preferences. Choose Edit > Preferences, then select the Invisible Elements category. Make sure the "Show section anchors when editing a page" option is checked, then click OK.

To link to a section anchor:

1. Browse to the page from which you want to link to the page that contains the anchors.

2. Select the text or image you want to make into a link to the section anchor.

3. Choose Insert > Link > Browse to Web Page, or choose Browse to Web Page from the Link pop-up menu in the toolbar. The Insert Link dialog appears.

4. Click the Browse button. The Browse to Link dialog appears. This dialog is actually a Web browser, and works like any other browser window. Use the dialog to browse to the page you want to link to. When the page you want is displayed, click OK.

   The Web address of the page you will be linking to appears in the "Web address (URL)" field of the Insert Link dialog (**Figure 6.14**).

5. Click the Advanced button to expand the dialog.

6. From the "Section anchor" pop-up menu, choose the anchor you want to use (**Figure 6.15**).

7. Click OK.

✔ Tip

- If the page that contains the anchor is on one of your draft pages, choose Insert > Link > Drafts and Recent Pages in step 3.

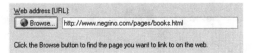

Figure 6.14 The page that contains the section anchors appears in the "Web address (URL)" field.

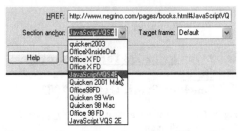

Figure 6.15 Choose the anchor you want to use from the "Section anchor" pop-up menu.

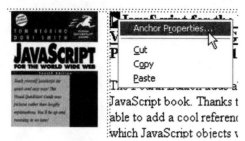

JavaScript book. Thanks t
able to add a cool referenc
which JavaScript objects v

Figure 6.16 Edit the section anchor's name by changing the Anchor Properties.

To modify an anchor:

1. Select the anchor on the page you're editing.

2. Right-click the anchor's flag icon.

   The anchor shortcut menu appears (**Figure 6.16**).

3. If you want to rename the anchor, choose Anchor Properties from the shortcut menu. The Edit Section Anchor dialog appears. Change the name, then click OK.

   To delete an anchor, select its icon and press the (Bksp) or (Del) key.

✔ Tip

■ You can also cut, copy, or paste named anchors using the anchor shortcut menu.

ADDING AND EDITING ANCHORS

Editing and Removing Links

It is a regular part of a site's maintenance to change or delete links. Contribute uses the Insert Link dialog to modify links, as well as to create them.

To edit a link:

1. Browse to the page where you want to edit links, and click the Edit Page button.

2. Right-click the link you want to edit. From the resulting shortcut menu, choose Link Properties.

   The Insert Link dialog opens.

3. Use the Browse button or the HREF field in the Advanced section of the Insert Link dialog to change the link's destination.

4. Click OK.

To remove links:

1. Browse to the page where you want to edit links, and click the Edit Page button.

2. Right-click the link you wish to edit. From the resulting shortcut menu, choose Remove Link.

   Contribute removes the link.

✔ Tip

■ Contribute doesn't ask for confirmation before it removes the link, so if you make a mistake and remove the wrong link, choose Edit > Undo or Ctrl-Z to get the link back.

CREATING TABLES

Top 10 U.S. Box Office			
As of October 2002			
Rank	Title	Cumulative Gross	Release Date
1	Titanic	$600,788,188	12/19/97
2	Star Wars	$460,998,007	5/25/77
3	E.T. The Extra-Terrestrial	$434,949,459	6/11/82
4	Star Wars: Episode I - The Phantom Menace	$431,088,295	5/19/99
5	Spider-Man	$405,692,151	5/3/02
6	Jurassic Park	$357,067,947	6/11/93
7	Forrest Gump	$329,694,499	7/6/94
8	Harry Potter and the Sorcerer's Stone	$317,557,891	11/16/01
9	Lord of the Rings: The Fellowship of the Ring	$313,364,114	12/19/01
10	The Lion King	$312,855,561	6/15/94

Figure 7.1 The HTML table format is perfect for tables with lots of data.

Tables on Web pages are often used to present *tabular information*—that is, data best presented in the form of rows and columns (**Figure 7.1**). But tables are also used as layout devices to help get around some of the limitations of HTML. Before tables were introduced for layout purposes, text and images were left-aligned on Web pages, and there was not a good way to arrange page elements.

When you use a table to lay out the elements of your Web page, you can put images next to text without worrying about the text's wrapping oddly around the image; create columns of text; and position different type treatments, such as headlines, body text, and figure captions, more precisely.

Contribute lets you create tables on your Web pages (unless, of course, your site administrator has disallowed their use), and tables will probably be an important part of the way you add content to your site. In this chapter, you'll learn how to use and format tables, ensure that tables and their content look the way you intend, and save time when you're using tables.

Creating a New Table

Tables typically consist of one or more rows and one or more columns. Each rectangular area at the intersection of a row and column is called a *cell*. Cells contain the page's text or images, and items within a cell can't extend past the cell's boundaries.

You can insert a table anywhere on a page, even within another table (this is called *nesting*). By default, Contribute creates tables with three rows and three columns, but you can easily change that format during the process of inserting the table.

If you can't create a table, your site administrator may have disabled this function. Check with the administrator if you have problems. If you're using a Macromedia Dreamweaver template as the basis of your page, you may not need to insert tables at all; the site designer may have created one or more editable areas in the template, which you fill with text or images. Designers often put editable areas inside tables they create; the Contribute user can't modify the table, which is being used as a layout device, but he or she can add to and edit editable areas within tables.

To add a table to your page:

1. Browse to and edit the page where you want to insert a table.

2. Place the insertion point where you want the table to appear.

3. Click the Insert Table button on the toolbar.

   or

   Choose Table > Insert > Table, or press ⌈Ctrl⌉-⌈Alt⌉-⌈T⌉.

   The Insert Table dialog appears (**Figure 7.2**).

Figure 7.2 Get started building a table with the Insert Table dialog.

Figure 7.3 You can set the width of your table either in pixels or as a percentage of the browser page width.

✔ Tips

■ If you're not sure how you want to use tables to lay out your page's elements, consider sketching out a map showing where things will go. It's usually easier to have a plan before you start creating tables and entering content.

■ To insert a table within a table, enter Draft mode, place the insertion point inside an existing table, and click the Table button on the toolbar. Nested tables offer even greater layout flexibility.

■ You don't have to get the number of rows and columns right the first time; you can always add or subtract them later. See the sections "Inserting Rows and Columns" and "Deleting Table Elements" later in this chapter.

4. Enter the number of rows you want in the table, and press `Tab`.

5. Enter the number of columns you want in the table.

6. Choose how you want to define the table's width (**Figure 7.3**). Selecting "Default width" creates a table with columns that are 200 pixels, or approximately 16 spaces, wide. If you want a different table width, select "Specific width," and then enter a number in the text box. Choose the units (either pixels or percent of the page width) of the width you enter using the pop-up menu to the right of the text box.

7. Set one or more (or none) of the following (see the "Table Anatomy" sidebar for explanations of these settings):

▲ Enter a figure in the "Border thickness" text box for the size of the border, in pixels, that will be displayed between cells.

▲ Enter a figure in the "Cell padding" text box for the amount of space, in pixels, between the content and the cell border.

▲ Enter a figure in the "Cell spacing" text box for the number of pixels of space between cells.

8. Choose the kind of header you want: None, Left, Top, or Both. The icons for the headers show you what each choice looks like.

9. Click OK.

The table appears in your draft page.

CREATING A NEW TABLE

Table Anatomy

Besides rows and columns, tables have several other attributes that affect how they look:

Border thickness is the width of the border around the table, in pixels (**Figure 7.4**). Contribute sets it to zero by default, which results in no border. If the border thickness is set to a nonzero amount, you will also see a border between table cells. You set the border thickness to zero when you're using tables for page layout.

Cell padding is the amount of space, in pixels, between a cell's borders and its content (**Figure 7.5**). Use this setting to give cell content more breathing room within cells.

Cell spacing is the amount of space between each table cell, also measured in pixels (**Figure 7.6**). Wide cell spacing gives the table a look that's very 1996, so use this setting with care.

Border color is the color of the border around the table and between the table's cells.

Background color is the color of the cell's contents (though you can set the color of text in the cell separately). You can also use the Text Color attributes to color text within the cell.

Table header tags part of the table as a header. The header is formatted as bold and centered, but more important, it has the <th> HTML tag, which allows screen readers used by visually disabled users to correctly read the table. It's better to use a table header tag in Contribute than to manually make cells bold and centered.

Sales Territory	1st Quarter (00)	2nd Quarter (00)
North	$2300	$2800
East	$5750	$5200
South	$3100	$3600
West	$8250	$7550

Sales Territory	1st Quarter (00)	2nd Quarter (00)
North	$2300	$2800
East	$5750	$5200
South	$3100	$3600
West	$8250	$7550

Sales Territory	1st Quarter (00)	2nd Quarter (00)
North	$2300	$2800
East	$5750	$5200
South	$3100	$3600
West	$8250	$7550

Figure 7.5 Cell padding has been set to 5 pixels, which gives more air around the table contents.

Sales Territory	1st Quarter (00)	2nd Quarter (00)
North	$2300	$2800
East	$5750	$5200
South	$3100	$3600
West	$8250	$7550

Figure 7.4 The same table with a border thickness of zero pixels (top), 1 pixel (middle), and 10 pixels (bottom). Cell padding and cell spacing are set to zero.

Figure 7.6 Cell spacing of 5 pixels gives wide borders between cells—a dated look. The border is emphasized with a color to make it easier to see.

Figure 7.7 This table is selected. Around its edges it has a thick border with resize handles.

Figure 7.8 When the pointer changes to an arrow, the whole row can be selected.

Selecting table elements

To work effectively with a table, you'll need to know how to select its elements. You can select an entire table; one or more rows and columns; an individual cell or multiple cells; and nonadjacent cells, rows, or columns.

To select the entire table:

◆ Click the bottom or the right edge of the table.

or

◆ Click the table's upper-left corner.

or

◆ Click in the table, and then choose Table > Select Table; or press ⟨Ctrl⟩-⟨T⟩.

A border with resize handles appears around the table (**Figure 7.7**).

✔ Tip

■ Right-clicking any interior cell border also selects the entire table.

To select an entire row:

1. Place the pointer at the left edge of a row. The pointer becomes an arrow.

2. Click to select the entire row (**Figure 7.8**). You can click and drag to select multiple rows.

To select an entire column:

1. Place the pointer at the top edge of a column.

   The pointer becomes an arrow.

2. Click to select the entire column (**Figure 7.9**).

   You can click and drag to select multiple columns.

Figure 7.9 The pointer also changes to an arrow when you select columns.

To select a single cell:

◆ Click and drag in the cell.

   or

   Click in the cell, then choose Edit > Select All, or press Ctrl-A.

To select multiple cells:

◆ Click in the first cell you want to select, and drag to the last cell.

   or

   Click in the first cell you want to select, hold down Shift, and then click in the last cell. You can also Shift-click in this manner to select rows or columns.

To select nonadjacent cells:

◆ Click in the first cell, hold down Ctrl, and then click the other cells you want to select. You can also Ctrl-click to select rows or columns.

Figure 7.10 You can resize columns numerically in the Table Properties dialog.

Resizing table elements

You can resize tables horizontally or vertically, and also make columns wider and rows taller.

To resize an entire table:

1. Click the bottom or the right edge of the table. The table is selected, and a border with resize handles appears around it.

2. Drag one of the resize handles. To widen the table, drag the handle on the right edge of the table; to make the table taller, drag the handle on the bottom edge of the table; and to make the table grow in both directions simultaneously, drag the handle at the bottom-right corner of the table.

To resize columns:

1. Select the column you want to resize.

2. Drag the column's right border.

   or

   Click the Table button on the toolbar. The Table Properties dialog appears, with the Table Column Properties tab selected (**Figure 7.10**). Enter a number in the "Column width" text box, and then choose either pixels or percent for the units from the pop-up menu. Alternatively, select "Fit to contents"; this makes the column resize to fit the contents.

To resize rows:

1. Select the row you want to resize.

2. Drag the bottom border of the row.

   or

   Click the Table button on the toolbar. The Table Properties dialog appears, with the Table Row Properties tab selected (**Figure 7.11**). Enter a number in pixels in the "Row height" text box, or click "Fit to contents," which makes the row resize to fit the contents.

✔ Tips

- If you set a width in percentage for a table, the table resizes based on the width of the user's browser window.

- Tables always stretch to fit the content inside the table.

- Text inside cells usually wraps to fit the width of the cell. To force the cell to expand to the width of the text, you can turn off text wrapping on a cell-by-cell basis. Ctrl-click in the cell, and then choose Table Cell Properties from the shortcut menu. Unselect the box next to "Wrap text," then click OK.

- Don't be misled into thinking you have ultimate control over row heights and column widths, and therefore control over what your site visitor sees. Different browsers display content differently, and short of previewing your site with every browser ever made on every computer platform, there's no way to be absolutely certain that your site visitor will see exactly what you intended.

Figure 7.11 You can also resize rows numerically in the Table Properties dialog.

Insert Row — — *Insert Column*

Figure 7.12 You can insert rows and columns quickly with the toolbar buttons.

Comedies	Tragedies
As You Like It	Hamlet
The Tempest	King Lear

Comedies	Tragedies
As You Like It	Hamlet
The Tempest	King Lear

Figure 7.13 A row has been selected in this table (top), and then a new row has been inserted above it (bottom).

Inserting Rows and Columns

Contribute allows you to add rows or columns to your table either singly or in multiples.

To insert a single row in a table:

1. Place the insertion point in a table cell.

2. Click the Insert Row button in the toolbar (**Figure 7.12**). A new row will appear below the row where the insertion point is.

   or

   Choose Table > Insert > Insert Row Above, or press Ctrl-M.

   or

   Choose Table > Insert > Insert Row Below.

   or

   Right-click in the cell, and choose either Insert Row Above or Insert Row Below from the shortcut menu.

   The row appears in your table (**Figure 7.13**).

✔ Tip

- If the insertion point is in the last cell of the table, pressing Tab adds a row to the bottom of the table.

To insert a single column in a table:

1. Place the insertion point in a table cell.

2. Click the Insert Column button in the toolbar. A new column will appear to the right of the insertion point.

   or

   Choose Table > Insert > Insert Column to the Left.

   or

   Choose Table > Insert > Insert Column to the Right.

   or

   Right-click in the cell, and from the shortcut menu choose either Insert Column to the Left or Insert Column to the Right.

   The column appears in your table.

To insert multiple rows or columns into a table:

1. Place the insertion point in a table cell.

2. Right-click, and then choose Insert Multiple Rows or Columns from the shortcut menu.

   or

   Choose Table > Insert > Multiple Rows or Columns.

   The Insert Rows or Columns dialog appears (**Figure 7.14**).

3. Select either the Rows or Columns radio button.

4. Enter the number of rows or columns you want to add. You can either enter a number into the text box, or use the arrow buttons next to the text box to increase or decrease the number.

5. Click the appropriate button to select the location of the new rows or columns.

   The rows or columns appear in your table.

Figure 7.14 The Insert Rows or Columns dialog allows you to add multiple rows or columns in one operation.

Deleting Table Elements

If you want to remove tables, rows, or columns, you can make short work of the task.

To delete a table:

1. Select the table by clicking its right or bottom edge. A border with resize handles appears around the table.

2. Press ⌷Bksp⌷.

To delete rows:

1. Select one or more rows.

2. Press ⌷Bksp⌷.

   or

   Choose Table > Delete > Row.

   or

   Right-click the row, and then choose Delete Row from the shortcut menu.
   The row disappears from the table.

To delete columns:

1. Select one or more columns.

2. Press ⌷Bksp⌷.

   or

   Choose Table > Delete > Column.

   or

   Right-click the row, and then choose Delete Column from the shortcut menu.
   The columns disappear from the table.

Formatting Tables

Contribute comes with 17 preset table formats, which apply fonts, cell borders, and cell-background colors to tables to provide a more attractive look (**Figure 7.15**). They are similar to features of Microsoft Excel's AutoFormat option for worksheets.

To apply table formatting:

1. Place the insertion point inside the table you want to format.

2. Choose Table > Format Table.

   The Format Table dialog appears (**Figure 7.16**).

3. From the Format list on the Basic tab, choose a format.

   A sample of the format appears in the dialog.

4. Click OK.

   The format is applied to the table (**Figure 7.17**).

✔ Tip

■ The preset formats only work on one table at a time. If you have nested tables, you'll need to apply a preset format to each table separately.

Sales Territory	1st Quarter (00)	2nd Quarter (00)
North	$2300	$2800
East	$5750	$5200
South	$3100	$3600
West	$8250	$7550

Figure 7.15 Using contrasting colors in rows (one of Contribute's preset table formats) can often make tables more readable.

Figure 7.16 The Basic tab of the Format Table dialog gives you 17 preset table formats.

Recipient	Gift	Purchased?
Sean	Playstation 2, games	No
Rachel	DVD player	Yes
Aaron	PS2 games	No
Brandy	Clothes gift certificate	Yes
Sierra	Gardening things	No
Robert	Educational software	No
Kayla	Doll house	Yes
Trinity	Toddler toys	No
Sophia	Baby toys	Yes

Figure 7.17 The preset format is applied to the table.

Figure 7.18 Use the color picker to remove colors as well as to apply them.

Saving Page Elements for Later Use

You can't create and save a custom table format in the Format Table dialog, but you can certainly create, format, and save an empty table for later use. This technique is also useful for saving other page elements you might want to use on more than one page.

First, create a new page on your site. On the new page, create a table, and then customize it with the Format Table dialog. Publish the page but don't link it to any other page on your site; that way, site visitors won't accidentally stumble upon it. When Contribute publishes the page, it switches back to the browser and displays the page with the formatted table. Finally, choose Bookmarks > Add Bookmark.

When you need to use the that table style again, use the bookmark to go to the page with the table, click Edit Page to create a draft of that page, copy the table, switch to the draft page where you want to use the table, and paste it in.

To remove the background colors from a table:

1. Select the table's cells (be sure not to select the whole table).

2. Right-click, and choose Table Cell Properties from the shortcut menu.

   The Table Properties dialog appears, set to the Table Row and Column Properties tab.

3. Click in the color box next to "Background color."

   The color picker appears (**Figure 7.18**).

4. At the top of the color picker, click the Default Color box (the square with a red slash through it).

5. Click OK.

   Contribute removes the background colors from the selected table cells.

Custom table formatting

Contribute lets you create your own custom table formatting, although unfortunately you can't name and save the custom format for later use from the Format Table dialog. The Advanced tab of the Format Table dialog gives you the control you need to quickly create and apply a custom table format.

To apply custom table formatting:

1. Place the insertion point inside the table you want to format.

2. Choose Table > Format Table.

   The Format Table dialog appears.

3. Select the Advanced tab (**Figure 7.19**).

4. Under "Table Properties," enter a number for the border width. If you don't want a border, enter 0.

5. In the "Left column" section, choose a text alignment and a text style from the pop-up menus.

6. Under "Header row," make any changes to the background color, text color, text alignment, and text style.

7. In the "Other rows" section, choose the row color. This will be your main row color.

8. From the "Alternate row" pop-up menu, choose how often you want alternate rows to be colored. Your choices are every other, every two, every three, or every four rows.

9. Choose from the Color pop-up menu for the alternate-row color.

10. Click OK.

    Contribute applies the new formatting to your table.

Figure 7.19 You can use the Advanced tab of the Format Table dialog to create your own table formats.

Figure 7.20 You can set the way text will wrap around your table in the "Table alignment" pop-up menu in the Table Properties dialog.

Setting Table Properties

Table properties apply to the entire table, and Contribute allows you to change the table's alignment and width, its border width and border color, its cell padding and cell spacing, and the background color for the whole table.

To set table properties:

1. Place the insertion point in the table you want to modify.

2. Choose Table > Table Properties, or press Ctrl-Shift-T.

   or

   Right-click in the table, and choose Table Properties from the shortcut menu.

   The Table Properties dialog appears (**Figure 7.20**).

continued on next page

Who's on Top: The Story of Formatting Precedence

Contribute allows you to set formatting for tables, rows, and cells separately, but some formatting is more important—here's the pecking order:

1. Cells

2. Rows

3. Table

Cell formatting takes precedence over row formatting, and row formatting takes precedence over table formatting. For example, if you set the background color for a single cell to green, then set the background color for the row that the cell is in to red, and then set the background color for the entire table to purple, neither the cell nor the row will change color, because their formatting preferences take precedence over those of the overall table formatting.

On occasion, you'll attempt to apply some sort of formatting to an entire table and it doesn't appear to work. Chances are, all the cells in the table had formatting applied to them at some time in the past, and because that cell formatting trumps the table formatting, the table format won't work until you change the cell formatting.

SETTING TABLE PROPERTIES

3. From the "Table alignment" pop-up menu choose Default, Left, Center, or Right.

   Each alignment has a different effect, as shown in **Figure 7.21**. There are also icons in the Table Properties dialog that show how the table will be aligned.

4. Make any other changes you want.

5. Click OK to apply the changes to your table.

✔ Tip

■ When you align the table to the right, a small placeholder icon appears in the left margin. This marks the beginning of the table on the page. It only appears on the draft page.

Sales Territory	1st Quarter (00)	2nd Quarter (00)
North	$2300	$2800
East	$5750	$5200
South	$3100	$3600
West	$8250	$7550

The quick brown fox jumps over the lazy dog. The quick brown fox jumps over the lazy dog. The quick brown fox jumps over the lazy dog. The quick brown fox jumps over the lazy dog. The quick brown fox jumps over the lazy dog. The quick brown fox jumps over the lazy dog. The quick brown fox jumps over the lazy dog. The quick brown fox jumps over the lazy dog. The quick brown fox jumps over the lazy dog. The quick brown fox jumps over the lazy dog.

Sales Territory	1st Quarter (00)	2nd Quarter (00)
North	$2300	$2800
East	$5750	$5200
South	$3100	$3600
West	$8250	$7550

The quick brown fox jumps over the lazy dog. The quick brown fox jumps over the lazy dog. The quick brown fox jumps over the lazy dog. The quick brown fox jumps over the lazy dog. The quick brown fox jumps over the lazy dog. The quick brown fox jumps over the lazy dog. The quick brown fox jumps over the lazy dog. The quick brown fox jumps over the lazy dog. The quick brown fox jumps over the lazy dog. The quick brown fox jumps over the lazy dog. The quick brown fox jumps over the lazy dog. The quick brown fox jumps over the lazy dog.

Sales Territory	1st Quarter (00)	2nd Quarter (00)
North	$2300	$2800
East	$5750	$5200
South	$3100	$3600
West	$8250	$7550

The quick brown fox jumps over the lazy dog. The quick brown fox jumps over the lazy dog. The quick brown fox jumps over the lazy dog. The quick brown fox jumps over the lazy dog. The quick brown fox jumps over the lazy dog. The quick brown fox jumps over the lazy dog.

The quick brown fox jumps over the lazy dog. The quick brown fox jumps over the lazy dog. The quick brown fox jumps over the lazy dog. The quick brown fox jumps over the lazy dog. The quick brown fox jumps over the lazy dog. The quick

Sales Territory	1st Quarter (00)	2nd Quarter (00)
North	$2300	$2800
East	$5750	$5200
South	$3100	$3600
West	$8250	$7550

brown fox jumps over the lazy dog. The quick brown fox jumps over the lazy dog. The quick brown fox jumps over the lazy dog. The quick brown fox jumps over the lazy dog. The quick brown fox jumps over the lazy dog. The quick brown fox jumps over the lazy dog. The quick brown fox jumps over the lazy dog. The quick brown fox jumps over the lazy dog.

Figure 7.21 The effects of different types of table alignment, set in the Table Properties dialog. From top to bottom, Default, Left, Center, and Right alignments.

Figure 7.22 The three cells at the top of this table (top) have been merged into one (bottom).

Figure 7.23 You can use the Split Cell dialog to divide cells into rows or columns.

Figure 7.24 In this example, the center cell has been split into four cells.

Merging and Splitting Cells

Contribute lets you combine two or more adjacent cells into one larger cell, or split a single cell into two or more cells.

To merge cells:

1. Select the cells you want to merge.

2. Choose Table > Merge Cells, or press `Ctrl`-`Alt`-`M`.

   or

   Right-click, and then choose Merge Cells from the shortcut menu.

   The cells merge (**Figure 7.22**).

✔ Tip

- You can merge an entire row or column into one cell.

To split cells:

1. Place the insertion point in the cell you want to split into two cells.

2. Choose Table > Split Cell, or press `Ctrl`-`Alt`-`S`.

   or

   Right-click, and then choose Split Cell from the shortcut menu.

   The Split Cell dialog appears (**Figure 7.23**).

3. Choose whether to split the cell into rows or columns.

4. Enter the number of new rows or columns for the split.

5. Click OK.

   The cell divides into two or more cells (**Figure 7.24**).

✔ Tip

- Even if you select multiple cells, Contribute can split only one cell at a time.

MERGING AND SPLITTING CELLS

Setting Cell Properties

Cell properties apply to the content of a single cell. You can set the cell content's horizontal or vertical alignment, set the cell's background color, or set whether or not the text wraps within the cell.

To set cell properties:

1. Place the insertion point in the cell you want to format.

2. Choose Table > Table Cell Properties.

    The Table Properties dialog appears, with the Table Cell Properties tab selected (**Figure 7.25**).

3. From the "Horizontal alignment" pop-up menu choose Left, Center, or Right (**Figure 7.26**).

Figure 7.25 The second tab of the Table Properties dialog changes depending on what is selected. Because a cell was selected, the tab shows Table Cell Properties.

Figure 7.26 Horizontal text alignment within a cell. From top to bottom, Left, Center, and Right text alignment.

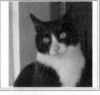

Figure 7.27 Vertical text alignment within a cell. From top to bottom, Top, Middle, and Bottom alignment.

4. From the "Vertical alignment" pop-up menu choose Top, Middle, or Bottom (**Figure 7.27**).

5. To change the cell's background color, click in the box next to "Background color" to bring up the color picker.

6. If you don't want the text in the cell to wrap, unselect the "Wrap text" check box.

7. Click OK to apply your cell formatting.

Sorting Table Contents

It's not uncommon to enter data into a table, then add more data, and then want to sort the whole thing. You asked for it, Contribute can do it. The program sorts by any column in your table, either numerically or alphabetically, in ascending or descending order, and can sort on two successive criteria.

There are some limitations to Contribute's sorting abilities. You cannot sort merged cells, and Contribute doesn't have the ability to sort part of a table, so you can't, for example, have the program ignore the merged cells you used for your table's title.

Another problem is that the sorting algorithm Contribute uses isn't terribly smart. For example, you can sort numerically, but Contribute doesn't understand dates in tables, so you're liable to get sorts like this:

5/19/99

5/25/77

5/3/02

Contribute sorted the dates numerically, reading left to right, which resulted in an incorrect sort.

Despite these restrictions, table sorting in Contribute is useful—you just have to be aware of them.

Figure 7.28 The Sort Table dialog lets you sort the contents of your table either alphabetically or numerically.

To sort a table:

1. Place the insertion point in any cell of the table you want to sort.

2. Choose Table > Sort Table.
   The Sort Table dialog appears (**Figure 7.28**).

3. From the "Sort by" pop-up menu choose the column you want to sort.

4. In the Order pop-up menu on the left, choose whether to sort the column alphabetically or numerically.

5. In the Order pop-up menu on the right, choose whether to sort the column in ascending or descending order.

6. If you want to sort on a second set of criteria repeat steps 3 through 5 with the "Then by" set of pop-up menus.

7. Make any selections from the Options list.

8. Click OK.
   Contribute sorts your table according to the criteria you selected.

✔ Tips

■ Contribute can't sort on rows, just columns.

■ If you want a merged row at the top of your table, do the sort first, and then merge the cells.

■ Be careful when you're sorting numbers. If you accidentally leave the sort on Alphabetically, you'll get an alphanumeric sort (1, 10, 2, 20, 3, 30) instead of a numeric sort (1, 2, 3, 10, 20, 30).

SORTING TABLE CONTENTS

USING DREAMWEAVER TEMPLATES

8

Macromedia Contribute is in some ways a bit of a paradox. Now that Web sites have become complex, requiring the skills of highly trained designers and Web programmers, Contribute returns to the content contributor the ability to change Web sites simply and directly. With Contribute, you can add to existing Web sites, but you can't create new sites. Contribute is a terrific tool for the novice, but it works best when using page templates created with Macromedia Dreamweaver, a complex program for Web professionals. Dreamweaver templates let Contribute users add content to pages without bringing down the wrath of the site designer if a mistake is made, and they allow everyone, from the administrative assistant to the Web expert, to make quick changes to Web pages knowing that the site will still look good and work well when they're finished.

In this chapter, you'll learn how to create new pages based on Dreamweaver templates; how templates can let you "fill in the blanks" without sacrificing good design; and how to create Sample Pages, the other kind of templates used in Contribute.

Creating New Pages from Dreamweaver Templates

Two kinds of templates are available to Contribute. The first are templates made in and saved from Dreamweaver, and are called, not surprisingly, *Dreamweaver templates*. The second kind, called *Sample Pages*, are Web pages made in other programs and saved for use in Contribute. For more information about using sample pages, see the "Building New Pages from Sample Pages" section in Chapter 3, or the section "Creating Sample Pages Templates" in Chapter 12, "Customizing Contribute."

A Dreamweaver template, which is placed on the Web site by the site administrator, provides a prebuilt page layout and includes a variety of page elements that will appear on all pages made from that template. This gives you a starting point for new pages. For example, a template could have a navigation bar and places for images and headings, plus places for body text. The page designer can designate these as *editable regions*, meaning that you can change them in Contribute. Other places on the page, *locked regions*, are not editable. Locked regions make it possible for designers to create templates that are ready for you to add content and that protect you from accidentally messing up the page design. When you put the pointer over one of the locked regions, it changes to the international symbol for "no" (the circle with a diagonal slash through it), and you cannot place the insertion point in the locked region.

✔ Tips

- You don't have to choose a template from the current Web site, though most of the time you'll want to do just that. You can instead choose a template in the New Page dialog from any of the sites for which you have a connection.

- Dreamweaver templates must be created in Dreamweaver 4 or later to work with Contribute.

- Contribute users can't create, delete, or edit Dreamweaver templates.

- Though Contribute works best when you have a network connection, you can use templates to create pages when you work offline. Contribute uses copies of the site's templates saved on your computer the last time you connected to the Web site. The program updates its copies of the templates and gets any new templates from the server when it starts up or when you edit the site connection.

- In most cases Contribute will also work with templates created in Adobe GoLive 6.0, since they follow the same standard as Dreamweaver templates.

Figure 8.1 The New Page dialog's Preview pane helps you select the correct template.

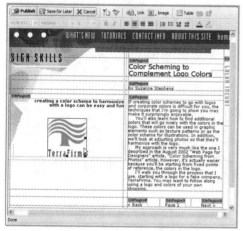

Figure 8.2 This new page contains a lot of information in the editable regions.

To create a page from a Dreamweaver template:

1. Browse to the Web site where you want a new page. It must be a site for which you have established a connection.

2. Click New Page on the toolbar.

   or

   Choose File > New Page, or press [Ctrl]-[N].

3. In the New Page dialog, click the small plus button next to Templates.

   The templates defined for your Web site appear.

4. Select a template to display it in the Preview pane (**Figure 8.1**).

5. Press [Tab] to highlight the "Page title" box, and enter a title for your new Web page.

6. Click OK.

   Contribute creates the new page based on the template (**Figure 8.2**).

   An editable region is marked in the draft page with a tab and a green outline.

✔ Tip

- Don't forget to link your new page to the rest of your site. See Chapter 6, "Working with Links," for more information about linking.

Dreamweaver Template Details

This section is meant for the Dreamweaver designer who will be creating templates for Contribute users, but Contribute users might also want to understand the details and constraints in creating templates.

Dreamweaver templates are available to Contribute users who have access to the site and who have permission to access particular templates. *Permission groups* are set by the Contribute site administrator, who can give one or more Contribute users access to specified templates. For example, the administrator could give users in a human resources department access to only that department's templates. See Chapter 10 for more information about site administration in Contribute, or Chapter 11 for more about administering Contribute sites from Dreamweaver MX.

Dreamweaver users can save any HTML page as a template. Dreamweaver saves templates with the filename extension `.dwt`, in a folder called Templates in the root folder of the site—attributes that Contribute recognizes. If the Templates folder doesn't already exist, Dreamweaver automatically creates it. Templates must be placed in the Templates folder to be correctly used by Contribute, so don't move templates to other folders. In fact, all kinds of problems can occur with templates if you change things (mainly they won't work correctly), so don't move the template files, don't move the Templates folder, and don't rename template files.

Automatic Updates

Pages based on Dreamweaver templates are automatically updated by Dreamweaver when a template changes. So you could, in principle, work on a page, and then work on it again at another time, and the page might look entirely different if the page designer had modified the template in the meantime.

The advantage of templates is that designers don't have to go through dozens or hundreds of pages to update the look of a site; all they need to do is change the templates. Templates are also useful for updating page elements that aren't, strictly speaking, design-related. For example, the designer can update the copyright date on an entire site by simply changing the template file and then allowing Dreamweaver to ripple the changes through all the pages based on that template.

One thing to note is that a change to a template will only propagate to pages based on the template if the change is made in a locked region. Any changes made to an editable region will not be changed when the template is saved or updated.

When creating your templates, be sure to keep the target Contribute user in mind. This user is more familiar with Microsoft Word than with powerful (and complex) Web tools like Dreamweaver, so you should design the templates so that they are easily understood by nontechnical contributors and therefore make it easier to add content to the site. Consider doing one or more of the following:

◆ Clearly label the editable regions with names that describe what content they should contain.

◆ If you are setting up templates for use on an intranet or in a collaborative environment, such as a team Web site for a group of people working on a project, it is usually best to keep your template design very simple and give your users one or more large, blank editable regions to work with. You don't need to worry too much about the look of such templates, since they will be for internal company use; it's more important to keep them flexible and usable. Too many design restrictions will restrict the team members' ability to adapt the templates to their needs.

◆ Use text fonts consistently in your templates.

◆ If you give the contributor the ability to style text, use Cascading Style Sheets to define your text styles.

◆ Use descriptive names for the CSS text styles so that users will know what they are for. "Body text" is a good name; "modArial3" is not, even if you know exactly what it is.

♦ Unless it is necessary for users to style text, use Contribute's permission groups to disable this capability. If you unselect the "Allow users to apply styles" and "Allow users to apply fonts and sizes" options in the Styles and Fonts section of the Permission Group dialog, the user will not have access to the Style, Font, or Font Size menus in the toolbar.

♦ If you allow users to add images to templates, make sure they send the pages to you for review before they publish the page. Most Contribute users will not have the expertise or the software tools necessary to correctly prepare images for the Web—for example, properly resizing or compressing them. See the "Letting Coworkers Review Your Pages" section in Chapter 3 for more information.

♦ Create a set of instructions for the Contribute user that explain how to use your template, and then send the instructions via email. You'll save yourself time in the long run, because you won't have as many user mistakes to fix.

♦ Your site will be more useful if you create and include a separate style sheet designed for easy printing. Include a button in the locked portion of the template that the site visitor can use to access the print version of the page.

They Can't Touch the Code

Macromedia Contribute users not only can't view HTML source code from within the program, they are also restricted by default from deleting or altering script tags; server-side includes; code tags such as ColdFusion, JSP, ASP, ASP.NET, and PHPform tags; and form elements.

If you need to give some users the ability to modify this sort of code, you can do so by unselecting the "Protect scripts and forms" option in the Editing section of the Permission Group dialog. It's a good idea to create a separate permissions group for these privileged users.

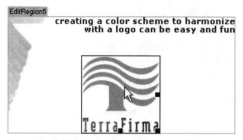

Figure 8.3 Editable regions are delineated by a green outline and a tab with the region's name.

Working with Editable Areas

Pages based on Dreamweaver templates show the editable regions in the draft window as areas outlined in green, with a tab and the editable region's name (**Figure 8.3**). Editable regions are most often containers for text, but they can also contain images, tables, and other objects, such as Flash movies. Editable regions do not have to be devoted to only one type of content; text and images can share a region.

If the site designer is using Cascading Style Sheet (CSS) styles, he or she can assign styles to each region, which will be used for any content you add. If the site designer has not used CSS styles, you can use HTML styles (if the site administrator has granted you text-formatting privileges).

To work in an editable area:

1. Create a new page based on a Dreamweaver template, or open a draft page created from a Dreamweaver template.

2. Click within the editable region's box, and add your content.

✔ Tips

- It's good practice for the Dreamweaver-template creator to give meaningful names to the editable regions. For example, different editable regions on a page might be named Headline, Byline, and Body Text.

- It can be very helpful for a template creator to give the Contribute user a printout of a mockup page with the editable regions labeled and annotated with a description of each region.

Repeating regions

A *repeating region* is a section of a template that the user can duplicate as often as needed in a template-based page. Repeating regions are most often used by designers to allow users to create as many rows of a table as needed, without the designer's having to specify the table size in advance. The designer only needs to create the first row of the table, and then the user can duplicate that row as he or she adds content. The repeating region contains controls to add a region, subtract a region, move a region down, or move a region up (**Figure 8.4**).

Technically, repeating regions in Dreamweaver must themselves contain editable regions as containers for content. It's possible for a repeating region to not contain an editable region, but then the user could not add any content.

To work in a repeating region:

1. Create or open a page based on a template that contains a repeating region.

2. Click within the editable regions in the repeating region, and make your edits.

3. Click the plus button to create another repeating region (**Figure 8.5**).

4. Make your edits within the new region.

5. (Optional) To rearrange regions, click in a region, and use the up and down arrows at the top of the repeating region to move it.

   or

   To remove a repeating region, click the minus button.

Add region —⌐ ⌐— Move region up

Subtract region —⌐ └— Move region down

Figure 8.4 You can easily create and manipulate repeating regions with these controls.

Figure 8.5 Clicking the plus button created the second instance of the repeating region (bottom). The second instance appeared with the same picture as the one in the top region, which is the placeholder image from the template. I then replaced the images.

Figure 8.6 The info bar lets you know when you have editable template properties.

Figure 8.7 You can edit the template properties in the Template Properties dialog. When selected, details about the available properties appear below the list, allowing you to modify them.

Setting Template Properties

Designers can create *optional regions* in templates that users can show or hide, depending on whether they are needed. Designers also have the option of letting users set the page's background color. Users can change either property with the Template Properties dialog.

To set template properties:

1. Begin editing a draft of the template-based page you want to change.

   The info bar lets you know that the template has editable template properties (**Figure 8.6**).

2. Choose Format > Template Properties.

   The Template Properties dialog appears (**Figure 8.7**).

3. Select a property in the Name list.

   Information about the property appears below the Name list.

4. Edit the property as needed.

   Depending on the property, different information appears below the Name list. If the property is a color, there is a color box that, when clicked, brings up the color picker.

5. Click OK.

SETTING TEMPLATE PROPERTIES

WORKING WITH EXTERNAL DOCUMENTS

Macromedia Contribute gives you the ability to edit Web sites, and in previous chapters we've seen how you can use Contribute to create and work with HTML files, image files, and even some media files, such as Macromedia Flash files. In Chapter 6, "Working With Links," we touched on Contribute's ability to link to other file types.

Contribute has special capabilities for working with documents from two other applications, Microsoft Word and Microsoft Excel. Contribute can create links to these documents; this merely uploads the files to your Web site, but better yet, you can import the contents of the documents directly into Contribute, turning that content into Web pages that you can then manage and edit within Contribute.

In order to import Word or Excel documents into Contribute, you'll need to have these programs installed on your machine. If you don't, you can still make links to the documents, but you won't be able to import or edit them.

Using External Documents

First, let's define our terms. For the purpose of this chapter, I'm calling a document that isn't created in Contribute, and isn't an HTML page, an *external document*. That's because when you attempt to edit these documents in Contribute, the program hands off the editing job to another application and refers to this task as Editing Documents in External Applications. You've already seen some of this external editing with image files in Chapter 5, "Working with Images," when Contribute called upon Macromedia Fireworks as an external image editor to modify a graphic.

Cleaner Office Documents

Recent versions of Microsoft Office, such as Office 2000 and Office XP, have the built-in ability to save Word and Excel documents as Web pages. You might be tempted to save a document from one of these applications as a Web page and then upload the page to your Web site. But when you use Contribute, you should resist the temptation, because Office documents imported into Contribute and then turned into Web pages end up being smaller in size (and therefore quicker to load), and compliant with accepted Web standards.

The problem is that when the Office applications save a document as a Web page, the HTML code created includes lots of excess or Microsoft-specific code that is designed to enable these Web pages to be brought back into Word or Excel more easily, but that most browsers don't need. This isn't a small amount of extra code, either; in test pages saved as Web pages from Word versus imported into Contribute, Word's resulting HTML files were as much as three times the size of Contribute's files.

Contribute's HTML-creation engine is based on Macromedia Dreamweaver's engine, and therefore Contribute inherits Dreamweaver's excellent ability to write clean, standards-compliant code. Standards compliance is important because compliant pages display well in any modern browser, whether that browser is running on a Windows machine, a Macintosh, or even a PDA or cell phone. Standards-based Web sites are also better for people with disabilities, especially the vision impaired who use audio screen readers or greatly enlarged text. Depending on where you're working, standards compliance may even be the law; many government agencies are now required to make their site accessible for people with disabilities. For more information about legal requirements for accessibility, see Section508.com (www.section508.com), named for the section of the 1998 Rehabilitation Act that established the federal accessibility requirements.

For more information about Web standards, visit www.webstandards.org, the Web site of the Web Standards Project, a volunteer organization that works to promote standards.

Contribute can either directly import the contents of a Word or Excel document, or upload a copy of the document to your Web site and create a link to it. See the "Linking to Local Files" section in Chapter 6 for more information about linking and uploading files. When visitors select the link, their Web browser downloads the file, which then needs to be opened in Word or Excel.

Contribute's import capability for Word and Excel documents offers a great way to make this content part of your Web site without requiring your site's visitors to own the Microsoft Office programs. You can drag and drop a Word or Excel document from the Windows desktop into Contribute, which will read this *source document*, convert it into HTML, and display it in Contribute's editing mode. You can then make any changes and publish the page to your Web site as usual.

When you import an Office document into Contribute, you are making a copy of the original document. Any changes you make within Contribute will *not* be reflected in the original Word or Excel document on your computer. Similarly, changes you make in Word or Excel to the original source document will not be reflected on your Web site. If you modify a source document and want to update your Web site, you need to delete the Web page with the now-superseded content, reimport the document into Contribute, and publish the new page.

Besides Word and Excel documents, Contribute is compatible with external documents in pretty much any format, such as Adobe Acrobat files, Microsoft PowerPoint presentations, MP3 music files, and Windows Media movie files. When you add one of these files to your Web site, Contribute uploads the file to the site and adds a link to the file. When a site visitor clicks the link, the file downloads to his or her computer.

✔ Tip

■ Contribute uploads files other than HTML documents to a folder on your Web site called **documents**. Contribute will create this folder if necessary, and will place it in the same directory as the page that contains the link to the external document.

USING EXTERNAL DOCUMENTS

Importing Word or Excel Documents

There are two ways to insert a Word or Excel document into Contribute. The easiest method is to drag and drop the file from the Windows desktop into Contribute's editing window. Alternatively, you can use commands in Contribute's Insert menu.

To import a Word or Excel document into Contribute:

1. Choose File > New Page, or press ⌈Ctrl⌉-⌈N⌉.

   or

   Browse to an existing page on your Web site, click the Edit Page button, and then place the insertion point where you want to add the imported content.

2. Drag the file from the Windows desktop into Contribute's editing window (**Figure 9.1**).

   or

   Choose Insert > Microsoft Word Document (or Insert > Microsoft Excel Document).

3. If you use one of the Insert commands, Contribute displays an Open dialog. Navigate to the document you want, select it, and click Open.

   The document's contents appear in the current draft.

   or

   If you dragged the document into Contribute, the Insert Microsoft Word or Excel Document dialog appears (**Figure 9.2**).

4. Choose to create a link to the document or to insert the document's contents into the current page, then click OK.

   Either the link or the document's content appears in the current draft (**Figure 9.3**).

Figure 9.1 Drag a Word or Excel file from the Windows desktop into Contribute's editing window to import the file.

Figure 9.2 The choice is yours: Add a link to the document file or add the document's content to the existing page.

Figure 9.3 The Word document is converted, and its content appears in the editing window.

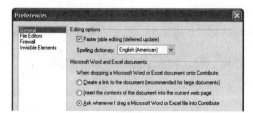

Figure 9.4 You can set a preference for how Contribute treats Office documents when you drag them into the program.

5. (Optional) Edit the document to suit the needs of your Web page.

6. Click Publish.

✔ Tips

■ You can set a user preference to have Contribute always either add the contents of the Word or Excel document or insert a link to the document. Choose Edit > Preferences, then select the General category. In the "Microsoft Word and Excel documents" section, select one of the three choices (**Figure 9.4**).

■ If the Insert > Microsoft Word Document or Insert > Microsoft Excel Document menu items are unavailable, it is probably because you don't have one or both of those programs installed. You can still get the content of the document into a Contribute draft page by having a coworker with the programs save the document as a text file, which you can then open with Notepad and paste into Contribute.

■ If you have inserted a link to a Word or Excel document, and your site's visitor has Word or Excel on his or her machine, clicking the link downloads the file and opens the application.

■ If an Office document is too large to import, you can work around Contribute's limitation by using Word or Excel to split the document into multiple smaller documents, and then import each document into its own new Contribute pages using Insert > Microsoft Word Document or Insert > Microsoft Excel Document. Then you can create links between the new pages.

■ If the document you dragged into Contribute is too large (greater than 300K when converted to HTML), Contribute displays a dialog that suggests you insert the file into your page as a link.

■ If you need to import a file that will be more than 150K of HTML, Contribute displays a warning that the import may take a while to process. The import will still work properly, but the program might appear to have stalled. Be patient; the page will appear when Contribute finishes the import. If the import is too big, Contribute lets you know with the dialog that suggests you add the Office document as a link.

■ Microsoft Office 97 does not have the ability to add the contents of a Word or Excel document by dragging and dropping it into Contribute. Instead, dragging and dropping always adds a link to the document. A partial workaround is to open Word 97 or Excel 97, copy the document's content to the Clipboard, and paste it into Contribute's editing window. Unfortunately, the pasted text will lose its text formatting.

Office Document Import Limitations

Contribute does a good job of importing many types of Office documents, but it has some limitations you should know about. The main limitation is that if the HTML file created from the Word or Excel document will be greater than 300K, Contribute inserts a link to the document rather than importing the document's content.

Word limitations. Besides the document size limit mentioned above, Contribute also has difficulty importing Word documents that have complex page layouts. For example, multiple-page Word documents that make use of text boxes for layout (**Figure 9.5**) often import as a single large image, usually missing the contents of the text boxes. Worse, the image does not look like the original page, and could have incorrect layout or even distorted type and images (**Figure 9.6**). You're better off creating complex layouts in Dreamweaver, saving them as templates, and inserting just the text and images in Contribute.

Figure 9.5 This desktop-publishing style Word document uses text boxes for layout control.

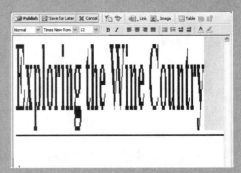

Figure 9.6 Importing complex layouts from Word into Contribute doesn't always give the best results. This file imported as a distorted image.

Figure 9.7 Excel files convert into complex HTML tables.

Figure 9.8 Pictures in the Excel file might mean distorted tables in Contribute.

A good rule of thumb is that if the document requires that you view it in Word's Print Layout View in order to see the page's elements, the document won't import well into Contribute (even Word itself doesn't do a good job of saving these kinds of documents as Web pages). This isn't a hard-and-fast rule, however, so it's usually worth at least attempting to import a Word document into Contribute that you think might be problematic. You might get lucky.

Excel limitations. When importing Excel worksheets into Contribute, the worksheet comes into Contribute as a complex table, with the worksheet's cells converted to cells in the HTML table (**Figure 9.7**). You can work with the imported table as you would any other table in Contribute (see Chapter 7, "Creating Tables"). If the Excel document contains an image (such as clip art), the image is placed into one cell in the HTML table, and the rest of the table cells resize to accommodate the picture (**Figure 9.8**), giving you perhaps unintended results.

Editing Imported Documents

Because an imported Word or Excel document has been converted into an HTML document in the process of importing it into Contribute, you edit it as you would any other Web page in Contribute.

Don't forget that the HTML document you are editing is a copy of the original source document, and changes you make in it will not be reflected in the original.

To edit an imported Word or Excel document:

1. Browse to the page you want to edit.

2. Click Edit Page in the toolbar, or choose File > Edit Page, or press Ctrl-Shift-E (**Figure 9.9**).

   The page appears in Contribute's editing window, and the page draft's name appears in the Pages panel of the sidebar.

3. Make the changes you want.

4. Click Publish to save your changes to the Web site.

Figure 9.9 Begin editing an imported Word or Excel document by clicking the Edit Page button.

Table 9.1

Preset File Editors		
FILE TYPE	FILE EXTENSION	PRESET EDITOR
Portable Network Graphics image	.png	Macromedia Fireworks
GIF image	.gif	Macromedia Fireworks
JPEG image	.jpg, .jpe, .jpeg	Macromedia Fireworks
Bitmap image	.bmp	Macromedia Fireworks
Text file	.txt	Notepad
XML file	.xml	Notepad
Word file	.doc	Microsoft Word
Excel file	.xls	Microsoft Excel
PowerPoint file	.ppt	Microsoft PowerPoint

Editing Other Document Types

To modify any content on your Web site other than an HTML file, you need to edit that content in the application in which it was created. For example, if you have a Macromedia Flash file on your site, you need to use the Flash application to modify it. But you have to use Contribute to begin the editing process so that Contribute keeps proper track of the edited copy of the file on your site. By using Contribute to manage the editing process, you can take advantage of Contribute's special features, such as rollbacks, which let you revert to a previous version of any published page or document. See Chapter 3, "Building Web Pages," for more information on rollbacks.

In order to edit a document in an external application, Contribute must know which application you want to use to edit a given file type. Contribute comes with a list of preset file types, as shown in **Table 9.1**, but you can add additional editing applications for each file type. You'll need to designate one application as the primary editing application for that file type.

For example, you might want to change Contribute's default file editor for image files, such as JPEG files. Contribute's default file editor for JPEG files is Fireworks. If you don't own Fireworks, you can add a different editor, such as Adobe Photoshop or even Windows Paint as the file editor of choice.

To add a file editor:

1. Choose Edit > Preferences.

   The Preferences dialog appears.

2. Select the File Editors category (**Figure 9.10**).

3. From the Extensions list, select the file extension for which you want to add a file editor.

4. Click the plus button above the Editors list.

   The Select External Editor dialog appears (**Figure 9.11**).

5. Navigate to the program you want to use as a file editor, select it, and click Open.

   The new editor appears in the Editors list.

6. (Optional) Select the new editor and click Make Primary.

7. Click OK to save your preferences.

✔ Tip

- If you have Dreamweaver MX installed, change the file editor for XML files from the default, which is Notepad, to Dreamweaver. The latter program's Code View has much better capabilities for editing XML files.

Figure 9.10 You can add file editors for any given file type.

Figure 9.11 Navigate to the editing application you want to use.

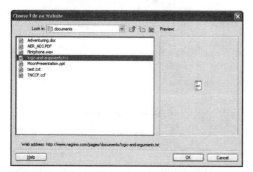

Figure 9.12 Select a file on your Web site for editing in an external application.

Figure 9.13 If necessary, the File Download dialog creates a temporary copy of the external file on your hard disk, so that it can be edited.

Figure 9.14 The File Placeholder screen tells you that Contribute can't display the type of file you've selected. Click Edit to launch the external file editor.

To edit an external document:

1. In Contribute's Browse mode, click the link to the external document you want to edit, or click Choose in the toolbar.

   The Choose File on Website dialog appears (**Figure 9.12**).

2. Navigate to the file you want to edit, select the file, and click OK.

   Depending on the type of file you are browsing, the File Download dialog may appear (**Figure 9.13**). If it does, click Open.

   If the file can be displayed by Contribute's browser, it will appear. Otherwise, the File Placeholder screen will appear (**Figure 9.14**).

continued on next page

EDITING OTHER DOCUMENT TYPES

3. Click Edit in the toolbar.

Contribute creates a new draft page, displays the Editing Draft in Another Application screen (**Figure 9.15**), and launches the file editor listed in Contribute's preferences for the kind of file you're editing (**Figure 9.16**).

4. Edit the file in the external file editor. When you are finished, save and close the file, then return to Contribute.

5. Contribute will still be displaying the Editing Draft in Another Application screen. Click the Publish button to save the draft page to the server.

✔ Tip

- If the Edit button is not available in step 3, check Contribute's Preferences to see if you have set a file editor in the File Editors category for the kind of file you're editing.

Figure 9.15 Contribute creates a draft page, tells you that it has handed the file off to an external editor, then switches to that editor.

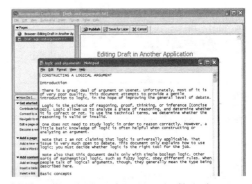

Figure 9.16 Make your changes to the file in the external editor, then save and close it before returning to Contribute.

SITE ADMINISTRATION

10

Site administrators manage Contribute Web sites. They do this mainly by controlling who has access to the site and by specifying the editing capabilities of the content creators using Contribute. Contribute users can be designated as site administrators, or sites can be administered using Macromedia Dreamweaver MX (version 6.1 or later).

As a site administrator, you'll be responsible for determining which users have editing access to your Web site, deciding the level of editing access (called *permissions*) of each user, and creating and distributing connection keys to your site's users. You'll typically define *permission groups* for your site, and assign individual contributors to a group. The permissions you assign to a group determine the nature of the editing access that members of the group have on your site.

In this chapter you'll learn how permissions work; how to become a site administrator; and how to create and modify sets of permissions you can assign to groups of users.

Becoming an Administrator

Contribute contains all the tools you need to become a site administrator, define and set permission groups, and send connection keys to site contributors. You can also administer Contribute Web sites using Dreamweaver MX 6.1 or later. See Chapter 11, "Managing Sites with Dreamweaver," for more information. Permission settings are stored on the server in the *shared settings file*, which is read by all Contribute users of the site. When an administrator is created for a site, Contribute (or Dreamweaver) creates the shared settings file, as well as several other files and folders it uses to maintain its Website management.

You can become the administrator of any Web site that doesn't already have an administrator. To see if a Web site has a current administrator, choose Edit > My Connections, and look for the Web site in the list in the My Connections dialog (**Figure 10.1**). The list shows the email address of the administrator, if one exists, or shows <No administrator> if one does not.

Figure 10.1 Sites without administrators show <No administrator> in the My Connections dialog.

Figure 10.2 Answer affirmatively when Contribute asks if you want to become the site's administrator.

Figure 10.3 You need to enter and confirm a new password to become a site administrator.

Figure 10.4 The Administer Website dialog allows you to apply settings for the entire site, add and maintain permission groups, and send connection keys.

To become a site administrator:

1. Choose Edit > Administer Websites, then choose the site you want to administer from the cascading menu.

   Contribute checks the site, and if the site does not have an administrator, it asks if you want to become the administrator (**Figure 10.2**).

   (If the site already has an administrator, you'll be prompted for the administrator's password. Since you want to become the site's administrator, you've made a mistake and should click Cancel in the password dialog.)

2. Click Yes.

   The Administrator Password dialog appears (**Figure 10.3**). Because you are adding administration to the Web site, the "Old password" field is disabled.

3. Enter a password in the "New password" field, and then enter it again in the "Confirm new password" field.

   If your two entries don't match, Contribute alerts you and allows you to reenter the confirmation password.

4. Click OK.

   The Administer Website dialog appears (**Figure 10.4**).

5. Make changes to sitewide settings or permission groups, as detailed later in this chapter.

   You can also send connection keys to users from this dialog.

6. Click OK to save your administrative changes.

✔ Tips

■ You must have already created a connection to a site before you can become its administrator.

■ If the Administer Websites menu is disabled, you might be working offline. Check to see if the File > Work Offline menu choice is active; if it is, select it to toggle Contribute back to online status.

■ You can send connection keys to coworkers via email from the Administer Website dialog. See "Sharing Site Connections" in Chapter 2 for details.

■ You can use a Web-based mail program, such as Hotmail, to send connection keys, but it isn't recommended. If you want to use a Web-based mail program, save the connection key on your computer and manually attach the file to the outgoing email message.

■ Contribute connection keys are XML files that are encrypted using 128 bit encryption, the same level of encryption used by Web browsers for e-commerce and online banking. It's possible to compromise this type of encryption, but it takes a lot of time and computing resources, making it effectively impractical. For most purposes, connection keys you send via email are secure. Just make sure you transmit the user's password separately from the connection key. A different email, fax, or phone call all work well.

Figure 10.5 Enter the administrator password to gain access to the Administer Website dialog.

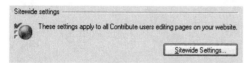

Figure 10.6 The "Sitewide settings" section of the Administer Website dialog.

Figure 10.7 You can change the administrator password in the Sitewide Settings dialog.

Figure 10.8 To change the administrator password, you'll need to enter the old password and then enter the new password twice.

Assigning Sitewide Settings

Sitewide settings are administrative settings that affect the Web site's general administration and all the Contribute users who connect to the site.

Changing administrator email and password

If you are the administrator of a Web site and you want to pass the responsibility on to someone else, you'll need to change the administrator's email contact address and the administrator password for the site.

To change the administrator contact or password:

1. Choose Edit > Administer Websites, and then choose the Web site you want to change from the cascading menu.

   The Administrator Password dialog appears (**Figure 10.5**).

2. Enter the administrator password, then click OK.

   The Administer Website dialog appears (**Figure 10.6**).

3. Click Sitewide Settings.

   The Sitewide Settings dialog appears (**Figure 10.7**).

4. Enter the email address for the new administrator.

   or

   Click Change Password. In the Change Administrator Password dialog (**Figure 10.8**), enter the old password and the new password, and then type the new password again to confirm. Click OK to return to the Sitewide Settings dialog.

5. Click OK to save your administrative changes.

✔ Tips

- If you can't choose a Web site from the Administer Websites cascading menu, it might be disabled. Choose Edit > My Connections, and then look at the Web site's entry in the My Connections dialog. If the Web site icon has a red slash through it, select the Web-site connection and click the Enable button.

- If you forget the administrator password, there's no way to get it back. You can, however, eliminate the password from the site by deleting it from the shared settings file using Dreamweaver or any text editing program (you can't do it with Contribute). Deleting the password from the shared settings file resets the site password to *blank*—that is, there will be no password for the site. To do this, open the root folder of your Contribute Web site and find the folder named _mm (for security reasons, you should use the server's file system to allow the Contribute users read-only access to the _mm folder, and you, the administrator, must have read and write privileges). Inside the _mm folder you'll find a file named `contribute.xml`, which is the shared settings file. Open the file in Dreamweaver, and look for `<admin_password value='xxxxxxxx' />` in the file. Delete the encoded string that is listed between the single quotes, signified by xxxxxxxx above. Then save the shared settings file back to the Web server. After this is done, you can once again administer your Contribute Web site. Go to Edit > Administer Websites as you would normally, only this time do not enter a password in the Administrator Password dialog before clicking OK. You should be sure to re-create an administrator password as described in this section.

- From a security standpoint, it's a good idea to periodically change the administrator password.

Figure 10.9 The Rollbacks section of the Sitewide Settings dialog allows you to set up to 99 rollback versions (but you probably don't want that many).

Enabling Rollbacks

Contribute can maintain up to 99 previous versions of each Web page on your site. For more information about how you can use rollbacks to revert to previous versions of your Web pages, see "Rolling Back to Previous Page Versions" in Chapter 3.

By default, Contribute saves three rollback versions of each page. Before you increase this number, you need to consider the effects of an increase on the amount of disk space your site will take up on your Web server, because the rollback versions of the pages, plus any associated files such as images, are saved on the server in a special folder called _baks.

To enable or change the number of rollbacks:

1. Choose Edit > Administer Websites, and then choose the Web site you want to change from the cascading menu.
   The Administrator Password dialog appears.

2. Enter the administrator password, then click OK.
   The Administer Website dialog appears.

3. Click Sitewide Settings.
   The Sitewide Settings dialog appears.

4. In the Rollbacks section (**Figure 10.9**), select the "Enable rollbacks" check box to make rollbacks active, or unselect it to turn rollbacks off.

5. If rollbacks are enabled, enter a number in the "Keep previous versions of each page" text box, or use the arrow buttons to set the number of rollbacks.

6. Click OK to return to the Administer Website dialog.

7. Click OK to save your administrative changes.

Index and URL mapping

When you start Contribute, it connects to your Web sites and looks for a number of items that help it determine the configuration of your Web server. One of the things Contribute needs to find is the *index page* for the site, which is the Web page that is displayed by default when a visitor browses to the site. For example, if you enter the address `http://www.peachpit.com/` into a browser, the page that is displayed may actually have the URL `http://www.peachpit.com/index.html`. Web servers are set to present the index page for a site when a visitor doesn't specify a page in the Web site. The Web server defaults to the index page rather than present the user with a "page not found" error message.

The most common default index-page file-names are

> `index.html`
>
> `index.htm`
>
> `default.html`
>
> `default.htm`

There are many other possible default index filenames, and Contribute comes with a list of 28 names. The program works through these names sequentially when browsing a Web server. If this list is not enough, you can add your own default index filenames, and you can also reorder the list if you want.

Contribute can also handle *alternate Web-site addresses*. For example, the Web server may be set to send a visitor to the default index page whether the visitor browses to either `http://www.peachpit.com/` or `http://peachpit.com/`. Contribute maintains a list of alternate Web-site addresses so that it knows the different addresses refer to the same site. The address doesn't have to be

Figure 10.10 Use the Index and URL Mapping dialog to fine-tune the index pages and Web sites that Contribute looks for.

✔ Tip

■ Some Web sites use port numbers to choose between different versions of a site. For example, a Web site that has localizations for different languages might have one language's Web site at `www.mysite.com` and the other at `www.mysite.com:8080`. A Web address that uses a different port number is considered by Contribute to be a different Web site. If you want Contribute to treat two Web addresses with different port numbers as the same site, you must add these Web addresses to the "Alternate website addresses" text box.

similar for Contribute to understand that it is the same site; for example, you can configure Contribute to recognize an entirely different domain, say `http://www.reallygood-books.com/`, as the same site as `http://www.peachpit.com/`.

To change index or URL mapping:

1. Choose Edit > Administer Websites, and then choose the Web site you want to change from the cascading menu.

   The Administrator Password dialog appears.

2. Enter the administrator password, then click OK.

   The Administer Website dialog appears.

3. Click Sitewide Settings.

   The Sitewide Settings dialog appears.

4. In the Advanced options section of the dialog, click Index and URL Mapping.

   The Index and URL Mapping dialog appears (**Figure 10.10**).

5. In the "Index files" section, use the Add, Edit, and Remove buttons or the up and down arrows to make changes to the "Index files" list.

   or

   In the "Alternate website addresses" section, use the Add, Edit, and Remove buttons to make changes.

6. Click OK to return to the Sitewide Settings dialog.

7. Click OK to return to the Administer Website dialog.

8. Click OK to save your administrative changes.

Removing administration

You can remove Contribute administration from the Web site. Removing administration deletes the sitewide settings file, and therefore also deletes all the permission groups from the site.

Figure 10.11 Contribute wants to make sure you're serious about removing administration from a Web site.

To remove administration from a Web site:

1. Choose Edit > Administer Websites, and then choose the Web site you wish to change from the cascading menu.
   The Administrator Password dialog appears.

2. Enter the administrator password, then click OK.
   The Administer Website dialog appears.

3. Click Sitewide Settings.
   The Sitewide Settings dialog appears.

4. In the "Advanced options" section of the dialog, click Remove Administration.

5. Contribute displays two successive warning alerts asking if you're sure you want to remove administration for the site (**Figure 10.11**).

6. Click Yes to both warnings.
   The Administer Website dialog closes.

✔ Tips

- Removing administration does not remove the rollback files or the Design Notes (files that are accessible to Dreamweaver users). In order to delete these items from a site, you must use Dreamweaver or an FTP program.

- Removing administration is not the same as removing the connection. If you want to delete the connection, choose Edit > My Connections, select the connection in the My Connections dialog, and click Remove.

- Whether you want to remove administration or remove the connection, be sure to publish or cancel any draft pages from that Web site first.

Figure 10.12 You begin assigning permissions in the Administer Website dialog.

Figure 10.13 Select the group for which you want to assign or change permissions.

Assigning Permissions

Contribute users can't choose which permission group they belong to. Rather, users are assigned to permission groups by the site administrator. By default, Contribute supplies two permission groups for each Web site: Administrator and Users. Generally speaking, the Administrator group has more control over the Web site than the Users group. For example, the Administrator group, by default, has the ability to delete pages, and the Users group does not. You can redefine the default permissions of each group. In this section, we'll explore the permissions you can assign.

Contribute assigns many permissions by default, and in many cases you may find that these defaults work well. On the other hand, if you need specific control of your site, you can set permissions to be as loose or as restrictive as you like.

You can also create and change your own permission groups, of course. See the "Creating Permission Groups" and "Modifying Permission Groups" sections later in this chapter for more information.

To assign permissions to a group:

1. Choose Edit > Administer Websites, and then choose the Web site you want to administer from the cascading menu. The Administrator Password dialog appears.

2. Enter the password and click OK. The Administer Website dialog appears (**Figure 10.12**).

3. In the "Permission groups" section of the dialog, select the group for which you want to assign permissions (**Figure 10.13**).

continued on next page

ASSIGNING PERMISSIONS

4. Click Edit Group.

The Permission Group dialog appears (**Figure 10.14**).

5. Select a category from the list on the left side of the Permission Group dialog.

The right side of the Permission Group dialog changes to reflect your choice.

6. Make changes to the permissions in the category you selected.

For details on each of the permissions within each category, see the discussion of each category below.

7. (Optional) If you wish, select another category, and then make changes to those permissions. Repeat until you're finished.

8. Click OK to save your changes to the permission group and return to the Administer Website dialog.

9. Click OK to save your permission changes to the server.

Permission categories ⎤   Permissions ⎤

Figure 10.14 The Permission Group dialog has several categories, each with a number of permissions you can set.

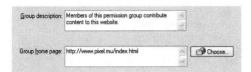

Figure 10.15 The General category contains information for permission-group members and sets the home page for the group.

General permissions

The first item in this category provides information for prospective group members, and the second sets the home page for the group (**Figure 10.15**).

- ◆ **Group description** is a field where you can clearly describe the responsibilities and permissions available for the group.

- ◆ **Group home page** allows you to enter a specific page within the Web site that will be the initial page for the group, and that can be different from the site's main home page. For example, if the home page of your site is http://www.backupbrain.com/index.html, and you want the sales team to default to the sales portion of the site, you can enter the URL http://www.backupbrain.com/sales/index.html in the "Group home page" text box. You can also use the Browse button next to the "Group home page" field to find the home page you want.

Folder/File Access permissions

These settings allow you to specify the folders to which users have access, as well as assign the ability to delete files on the site.

◆ **Folder access** lets you give users permission to edit files in any folder on the Web site, or restrict them to editing only in specified folders (**Figure 10.16**). The default is to allow users to edit files in any folder. If you want to restrict folder access, select "Only allow editing within these folders," and then click Add Folder, which brings up the Choose Folder dialog. Navigate to the folder you want users to be able to edit, and then click the Select button, which returns you to the Permission Group dialog and adds the selected folder to the folder list. Repeat as necessary to add other folders. To change one of the folders in the list, select it, and then click Edit or Remove.

◆ **File deletion** controls whether or not users can delete files they can edit (**Figure 10.17**). The default is to prevent users from deleting files and allow only members of the Administrator group to delete files. To enable file deletion for users, select "Allow users to delete files they have permission to edit." This enables the "Remove rollback versions on delete" option. You must select this option if you want your users to have the ability to delete files.

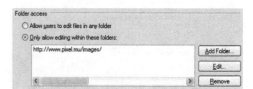

Figure 10.16 The "Folder access" section of the Folder/File Access permissions category lets you specify which folders users can access to edit files.

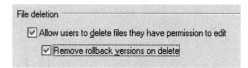

Figure 10.17 You can control whether users can delete files from the site.

Figure 10.18 The "Non-template pages" section of the Editing permissions category controls what users can accomplish on non-Dreamweaver pages.

Figure 10.19 You can control paragraph spacing using either CSS styles or HTML tags.

Editing permissions

Editing permissions control the actions users can take on nontemplate pages, how Contribute creates paragraph breaks, and other miscellaneous editing options.

◆ **Non-template pages** controls options for pages that aren't created from Dreamweaver templates (**Figure 10.18**). By default, Contribute is set to "Allow unrestricted editing" and "Protect scripts and forms." The first option lets users insert and modify anything on a Contribute page, including text, images, tables, Flash movies, and more. The exception is controlled by the second option, which prevents users from deleting script tags, code tags (such as instructions for Macromedia ColdFusion or ASP tags), and form elements. If you deselect this option, users will be able to modify code embedded in your Web pages. Most Contribute users will not have the knowledge or experience to change code safely, and the tools for code modification are far superior in Dreamweaver. In general, it's best to leave the Web programming to Dreamweaver users.

The "Only allow text editing and formatting" option restricts users to editing text, modifying styles, and creating bulleted or numbered lists. Users cannot add images, links, Flash movies, or tables.

◆ **Paragraph spacing** controls Contribute's behavior when the user presses [Enter] (**Figure 10.19**). The default uses CSS styles and moves the insertion point down one line when [Enter] is pressed. The other option moves the insertion point down two lines and uses HTML <p> tags. For a detailed explanation of the effects of these controls, see the "That's the Breaks" sidebar in Chapter 4.

◆ **Other editing options** includes four miscellaneous options (**Figure 10.20**). "Allow multiple consecutive spaces" uses the HTML   character (a nonbreaking space) to allow the user to insert multiple consecutive spaces between words. This option is turned on by default. If you turn it off, browsers will collapse multiple spaces into only one space.

The "Enforce accessibility options" choice is turned off by default, but I suggest you turn it on. When it is on, Contribute always prompts users for information that will make it easier for people with disabilities to access your Web site. For example, when the user inserts an image, Contribute prompts the user to provide a text description for the image (also known as ALT text), which can be read by screen readers used by site visitors with visual disabilities (**Figure 10.21**). This option does not require users to specify header elements for tables (although to learn how to employ proper accessibility, see Chapter 7, "Creating Tables," for more information about table header elements).

The "Use <strong> and <em> in place of <b> and <i>" option tells Contribute to use more up-to-date HTML when users format text as bold or italic. This option is turned on by default.

The "Line break type" pop-up menu allows you to specify the invisible Windows, Macintosh, or Unix line-break characters. Contribute defaults to Windows line breaks, but the line breaks used should be compatible with the type of line breaks your Web server understands. Check with your Web-site administrator if you have questions.

Figure 10.20 The miscellaneous editing options include the important ability to enforce accessibility requirements for site visitors with visual disabilities.

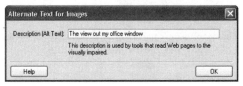

Figure 10.21 If you have enabled accessibility enforcement, Contribute presents this dialog whenever you add an image to your Web site.

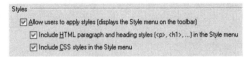

Figure 10.22 The Styles section of the Styles and Fonts permissions category controls whether or not the user can apply text styles.

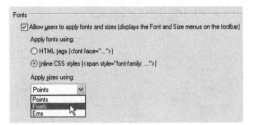

Figure 10.23 The Fonts section of the Styles and Fonts permissions category controls the user's ability to apply fonts and font sizes.

Styles and Fonts permissions

Styles and Fonts permissions control users' ability to apply text styles and define the kinds of text styles they can use. You can also allow or disallow users to specify fonts and font sizes.

◆ **Styles** has the "Allow users to apply styles" option turned on by default (**Figure 10.22**). The two subsidiary options are also turned on by default and allow HTML paragraph and heading styles and CSS styles to appear in the Style menu.

◆ **Fonts** lets you enable or disable the Font and Font Size menus on the Editing toolbar. This option is enabled by default. If you allow users to apply fonts and sizes, you have the further option of specifying whether fonts should be applied using HTML tags or CSS styles (**Figure 10.23**). If you choose CSS styles, you have the additional option of using points, pixels, or ems as the measurement unit.

✔ Tips

■ You can prevent a CSS style from being available to Contribute users by naming the style with the prefix mmhide. The style will not appear in the Style menu. For example, if you use a style named Slugline in your page, but you don't want Contribute users to be able to use that style, rename it mmhideSlugline.

■ You have the most control over the contributor's use of text on the site if you deselect "Allow users to apply fonts and sizes" and specify CSS styles within the editable regions on the template. On the other hand, this is so restrictive that your users may revolt.

New Pages permissions

The New Pages settings control the kind of Web pages users can create from the New Page dialog.

◆ **Allow users to** has three self-explanatory options that are enabled by default (**Figure 10.24**). They are "Create a blank page," "Use built-in sample pages," and "Create a new page by copying any page on the website." By selecting the "Create a new page by copying a page from this list" option, you can add or subtract pages from your Web site that can be used like Sample Pages, although they will appear in the Templates category of the New Page dialog. Use the Add button to add pages from your Web site to the list. You can only use pages from the current Web site; you can't select pages from any of your other Web sites for this list.

◆ **Use Dreamweaver templates** is enabled by default, as is its subsidiary option "Show users all templates." You also have the option of restricting the templates users can see by clicking the "Only show users these templates" button and moving templates from the "Hidden templates" list, using the Hide and Show buttons (**Figure 10.25**).

✔ Tips

■ By restricting the Dreamweaver templates that members of a group can see, you can prevent members of one department from accidentally using templates meant for another department. For example, by restricting templates for the public relations group to the templates designed for press releases, you can make sure the PR group doesn't accidentally use templates meant for the engineering group that are intended for progress reports.

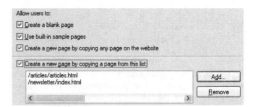

Figure 10.24 The "Allow users to" section of the New Pages permissions category controls the source of new pages in the New Page dialog.

Figure 10.25 You can restrict users to certain Dreamweaver templates.

■ If you don't like the Sample Pages that Macromedia provides with Contribute, you can prevent your users from accessing them by deselecting the "Use built-in sample pages" option.

Figure 10.26 Limit the maximum size of images that users can add to your site in the New Images category of the Permission Group dialog.

New Images permissions

The New Images category lets you restrict the maximum file size of images that users can add to the site's pages.

◆ **Maximum image file size** can be set to Unlimited, or you can enter a number, in kilobytes, in the "Limited to" text box (**Figure 10.26**).

✔ Tips

■ If you set the maximum image file size permission to 0, users won't be able to insert images. This is useful when you want users to be able to change text but not add graphics to the Web site.

■ Choosing a relatively low number for the maximum image file size prevents users from adding images to your site that will be too big for site visitors using dial-up connections to load in a reasonable amount of time.

ASSIGNING PERMISSIONS

Creating Permission Groups

You're not limited to the two default groups Contribute provides; you can create new groups as you need them. After you, as the site administrator, create permission groups, you'll need to send connection keys to your users. See "Sharing Site Connections" in Chapter 2 for more information.

Figure 10.27 Name the new permission group.

To create a new permission group:

1. Choose Edit > Administer Websites, and then choose the Web site you want to administer from the cascading menu.

   The Administrator Password dialog appears.

2. Enter the password and click OK.

   The Administer Website dialog appears.

3. Click New.

   The Permission Group Name dialog appears (**Figure 10.27**).

4. Enter a name for the new group, and then click OK.

   You return to the Administer Website dialog, and the name of the new group appears in the dialog.

5. Select the new permission group in the list, and then click Edit Group.

6. Edit the group's permissions as described in the "To assign permissions to a group" section earlier in this chapter.

✔ Tip

■ Individual permission groups don't have passwords, so it's not possible for a single user to be a member of more than one permission group. Users join a permission group by using the connection key sent to them by the site administrator.

CREATING PERMISSION GROUPS

Modifying Permission Groups

You can modify the editing privileges for groups, delete groups, or duplicate groups to use as the basis for new groups.

Because Contribute stores the permission-group settings in the *shared settings file* on the server, and each copy of Contribute reads that file when it starts up, you can change the permissions for any group at any time without having to send new connection keys to all the group members. You will, however, need to send users a new connection key if you move them into a different group.

✔ Tip

■ Contribute stores the shared settings file in a folder called _mm that resides at the root of the Web site. You can't see this folder from within Contribute.

To edit a permission group:

1. Choose Edit > Administer Websites, and then choose the Web site you want to administer from the cascading menu. The Administrator Password dialog appears.

2. Enter the password and click OK. The Administer Website dialog appears.

3. Select a permission group in the list, and then click Edit Group.

4. Edit the group's permissions as described in the "To assign permissions to a group" section earlier in this chapter.

To duplicate a permission group:

1. Choose Edit > Administer Websites, and then choose the Web site you want to administer from the cascading menu.

The Administrator Password dialog appears.

2. Enter the password and click OK.

The Administer Website dialog appears.

3. Select a permission group in the list, and then click Duplicate.

The Permission Group Name dialog appears.

4. Enter a name for the new group, and then click OK.

You return to the Administer Website dialog.

5. To edit the new group's permissions, click Edit Group, and then edit the permissions as described earlier in this chapter.

✔ Tip

■ Duplicating a group is useful if you have groups with similar but not identical permissions. For example, you might have two groups that need the same editing access but use a different template. You can create and tweak the permissions for the first group, then duplicate that group and only change the template sets for the second group. It's a big time-saver.

To delete a permission group:

1. Choose Edit > Administer Websites, and then choose the Web site you want to administer from the cascading menu.

The Administrator Password dialog appears.

2. Enter the password and click OK.

The Administer Website dialog appears.

3. Select a permission group in the list, and then click Delete.

Contribute asks you to confirm the deletion (**Figure 10.28**).

4. Click Yes.

Figure 10.28 Before you delete a permission group, Contribute asks if that's what you want to do.

✔ Tips

■ Be careful when you delete a permission group—you can't undo the delete action.

■ There's no way to remove a single user from a permission group. A workaround is to duplicate the group with a new name, send new connection keys to the users you want to include in the new group, and then delete the old group.

MANAGING SITES WITH DREAMWEAVER

Macromedia Contribute is designed around the principle that one or more site administrators will organize and maintain a Web site. Often these administrators are the people who created the Web site, using a production tool, such as Macromedia Dreamweaver MX, to build and prepare the site for use by content creators who employ Contribute.

Beginning with Dreamweaver MX 6.1, the tools to administer Contribute sites are built into Dreamweaver, so you can create and administer the site entirely within Dreamweaver. For the most part, these tools replicate the site-administration abilities built into Contribute, which are detailed in Chapter 10, "Site Administration." In this chapter you'll learn how to update Dreamweaver MX to administer Contribute; how to create a Contribute-friendly site structure in Dreamweaver; how to become the administrator of a Contribute site with Dreamweaver; and how to use Contribute-style rollbacks from Dreamweaver to revert to previous versions of pages on your site.

Updating Dreamweaver for Contribute

You must be running Dreamweaver MX version 6.1 or later to work with Contribute sites. You can download an updater on the Macromedia Web site (www.macromedia.com/downloads/). Versions of the updater are available for both Windows and Macintosh. Naturally, all new copies of Dreamweaver MX are the updated version.

The 6.1 updater adds three Contribute-related features to Dreamweaver:

◆ The ability to administer Contribute sites from within Dreamweaver

◆ The ability to create and send connection keys to Contribute users

◆ Contribute's page-versioning system, which allows you to roll back pages to previous versions, just as you can with Contribute

If you purchased Dreamweaver after December 2002, you should check to see whether you are running a Contribute-compatible version.

To check your version of Dreamweaver MX:

1. Launch Dreamweaver MX.

2. Choose Help > About Dreamweaver (Windows) or Dreamweaver > About Macromedia Dreamweaver MX (Macintosh).
   The Dreamweaver credits screen appears.

3. Click the credits screen once.
   The version screen appears (**Figure 11.1**). If the version shown is earlier than 6.1, you need to download and apply the updater in order to work with Contribute from Dreamweaver.

4. Click the version screen once to dismiss it.

—*Version number*

Figure 11.1 Check your version of Dreamweaver MX to make sure it is compatible with Contribute.

To update Dreamweaver MX:

1. Download the appropriate updater for your computer (either Windows or Macintosh) from Macromedia's Web site at www.macromedia.com/downloads/.

2. Double-click the updater program to launch it.

   The updater program searches your hard drive for an older version of Dreamweaver MX. When it finds the old version, the program prompts you to complete the update.

3. When the update is completed, exit the updater program.

✔ Tips

- Have a fast Internet connection or a lot of time before you download the Dreamweaver updater program—the Windows updater is almost 15 MB, and the Mac updater weighs in at almost 26 MB.

- Be sure to disable all extensions in Dreamweaver MX before installing the version 6.1 updater. Use the Extension Manager to do the job by choosing Commands > Manage Extensions from within Dreamweaver. If you install the updater while Dreamweaver MX extensions are enabled, the extensions will disappear from the Dreamweaver menus. After you install the updater and start Dreamweaver MX 6.1 for the first time, use the Extension Manager to reenable your extensions.

- The version 6.1 updater also fixes a long list of bugs (some minor, some not so) that Macromedia discovered in Dreamweaver 6.0, so it's a good thing to install even if you don't plan to administer Contribute sites from Dreamweaver. For a list of the Dreamweaver bugs fixed by the updater, check the Release Notes section of the Macromedia Dreamweaver Support Center on Macromedia's Web site.

UPDATING DREAMWEAVER FOR CONTRIBUTE

Building Sites for Contribute

Many Contribute site administrators will also be the designers or developers, and there are a variety of things you can do to make it easier for content creators to use your sites.

Preparing a Contribute-friendly site structure

It's a good idea to review your site structure and make any changes necessary to facilitate the creation of permission groups before you deploy Contribute to your content creators. For example, you might have a Web site with many contributors whose content doesn't affect the content of other users, such as a faculty Web site where each faculty member can update information about his or her class schedule, office hours, etc. For such a site, it might be appropriate to create and designate a separate folder for each faculty member. When you create the permissions for the site. You could create a single permission group in Contribute for all faculty members and use the server's file system to limit their server access so that each faulty member could only read and write to files in his or her own folder. Or if you want to handle access entirely within Contribute, you could create a separate Contribute permission group for each faculty member, specifying the folder he or she has access to in the Folder Access setting in the File/Folder Access category of the Permission Group dialog. Either way, such a site would have a single administrator, single shared-settings file, and a shared set of Dreamweaver templates (if the site uses Dreamweaver templates).

Contribute could also be deployed in sites with multiple administrators, one for each section of the site. Each administrator would set up his or her section for his or her Contribute users. For example, a company could have a different section (and a different administrator) for the sales department, the human resources department, the manufacturing group, and customer service. Each department would have its own folder, and each department could have its own set of Dreamweaver templates in the Templates folder within its section folder. The benefit of this approach would be that all the users in all the departments could browse the full site, but they would be restricted to editing only pages within their folders.

Building standards compliance into the site

Contribute shares the excellent Dreamweaver MX HTML-creation engine, a hidden bonus. You can create Web sites that are completely compliant with Web standards, as long as the designer has taken care to create compliant templates. Web standards help ensure that everyone has access to the information on your Web sites and make the browsing experience faster and more enjoyable, and they also make life easier for Web designers and developers.

Standards compliance facilitates the use of the Web by people with special needs; the degree to which a site can be fully used by people with disabilities is referred to as its "accessibility." On a standards-compliant Web site, blind people can have their computer read the Web pages. People with poor eyesight can have pages magnified for easier reading. The nondisabled also derive benefits—compliant sites enable people using handheld devices, such as PDAs or cell phones, to browse the Web as easily as users sitting at a desktop computer. And compliant sites can be easier for search engines to access, evaluate, and index, making for better search results for your site.

continued on next page

BUILDING SITES FOR CONTRIBUTE

Besides these practical reasons, there's another reason you might want to build standards-compliant Web sites. With the adoption of government-backed accessibility standards in the United States, the European Union, Canada, Australia, and Japan, accessibility might not just be a good idea—it could be the law.

Contribute offers several settings that allow designers and Contribute site administrators to establish and maintain accessibility. Once these settings have been activated, content creators must provide text descriptions for images (also known as ALT text). Contribute users can also easily identify the headings in tables used for tabular data. The administrator can also specify the use of CSS for text formatting. For more information about these accessibility settings, refer to "Other editing options" in the "Editing permissions" section and the "Styles and Fonts permissions" section in Chapter 10.

Dreamweaver MX has a wide variety of tools to help the page designer create standards-compliant, accessible templates that can then be used in Contribute:

◆ You'll find more than two dozen accessible templates built into Dreamweaver in the Page Designs (Accessible) category of the New Document dialog (**Figure 11.2**).

◆ Dreamweaver also has accessibility preferences; refer to the Dreamweaver documentation for more information.

◆ The Macromedia Accessibility page, at www.macromedia.com/macromedia/accessibility/, has a great deal of information on accessibility and Web standards, and many megabytes of additional accessible templates, free for the downloading.

◆ Dreamweaver offers several extensions that can help you evaluate and modify Web pages to be more usable and accessible. You can find links to these extensions on the Macromedia Accessibility page.

Figure 11.2 Dreamweaver comes with many accessible templates.

✔ Tip

■ The Sample Pages you find in Contribute's New Page dialog are all accessible, but they are not all standards-compliant (meaning that they do not necessarily pass as valid HTML when using the W3C HTML validator).

Figure 11.3 When you're working in Dreamweaver, the first time you access a site that Contribute users have worked on, Dreamweaver asks if you want to enable Contribute compatibility. (In this case, I accessed and administered the Contribute site using Dreamweaver MX in Mac OS X.)

Figure 11.4 You need to identify yourself as a Contribute user by entering your "Check Out Name" and email address.

Enabling Dreamweaver Settings for Contribute

If your remote site has previously been used by Contribute, Dreamweaver MX automatically detects that fact when it first connects to the site, and it asks if you want to enable Contribute compatibility (**Figure 11.3**). If you do, Dreamweaver changes a number of settings in the program and on the site. The program also shows the Contribute Site Settings dialog, which asks for your name and email address as a Contribute user (**Figure 11.4**).

When you fill out this dialog, be sure to choose a different check-in/check-out name for Dreamweaver than the one you use in Contribute so that Contribute (and Dreamweaver) can keep correct track of who is editing a page. If you're not familiar with the Dreamweaver terminology, the check-in/check-out name is the name that Dreamweaver (and now, Contribute) uses to identify the people who work on pages in a site. Because both Dreamweaver and Contribute check pages out of a site while they are being edited, you want to be able to keep track of which application has a page checked out.

Both the user name and email address are significant, because they are used together to create a unique user identity. If you prefer, you can use a different user name but the same email address in both applications. By utilizing different user names and having them be descriptive, you can immediately tell which application you used to check out the page. For example, I could set up my sites using "tom-dw" (for Dreamweaver) and "tom-con" (for Contribute), but the same email address (webteam@negrino.com). Then, if I have a page checked out in Dreamweaver and browse to that page in Contribute,

Contribute will notify me in its info bar that the page cannot be edited because it is checked out by "tom-dw <webteam@negrino.com >". I can use a single email address and still immediately know which program has the file in use.

You can see the settings Dreamweaver changes in the Contribute category of the Site Definition dialog (**Figure 11.5**). Here, Contribute compatibility is turned on, and the URL of the site root is automatically entered. There's also a button to open the Site Administration dialog, which is identical to the dialog of the same name in Contribute.

✔ Tips

- You can extend the user names you use in Contribute and Dreamweaver to identify the different machines you use, as well as the different applications. For example, if you use Contribute on both your laptop and your desktop machine, you could have the user names "tom-con-laptop" and "tom-con-desktop."

- You can use the Test button in the Contribute category of the Site Definition dialog to verify that you've entered the correct URL (if you did it manually) or that Dreamweaver has (if it was entered automatically). Dreamweaver connects to the Web site and verifies that it has the correct URL to administer the site.

Figure 11.5 Once you enable Contribute compatibility, Dreamweaver makes changes in the Contribute category of the Site Definition dialog.

Figure 11.6 Enter the site administrator's password to begin creating a connection key.

Figure 11.7 The Administer Website dialog looks much the same either in Windows or on the Macintosh (shown here).

Figure 11.8 Choose whether you want to send your FTP log-in and password along with the connection key.

Sharing Connection Keys

As a Dreamweaver user, you're quite likely to be the Contribute site administrator, so you need to know how to send connection keys to Contribute users. The process of sending connection keys is almost the same as it is in Contribute, with minor differences, depending on whether you're using the Windows or the Macintosh version of Dreamweaver MX.

Unfortunately, Dreamweaver MX does not import Contribute connection keys, so you can't use Contribute connection information to add Dreamweaver users to your Web site. Also, Dreamweaver users cannot be assigned to a group, so there's no way to restrict editing access, template access, or Web-site folder access for a Dreamweaver user.

To send connection keys from Dreamweaver:

1. From the menu bar in the Site window, choose Site > Administer Contribute Site (Windows) or Site > Administer Contribute Site (Macintosh).

    The Administrator Password dialog opens (**Figure 11.6**).

2. Enter the password, and click OK.

    The Administer Website dialog opens (**Figure 11.7**)

3. Click the Send Connection Key button.

    The first screen of the Export Wizard appears (**Figure 11.8**).

4. Make sure that Yes is selected, and then click Next.

    (Optional) Select the "Include my FTP login and password" check box. If you want to include your log-in information in the key, select this box; if the person to whom you're sending the key has his or her own FTP log-in, leave this option unselected.

continued on next page

If you choose No, Contribute allows you to customize the connection settings before you create the export file. See Chapter 10 for more information about customizing connection settings.

5. The Group Information screen appears. Select the permission group you want for the connection file you're creating, then click Next.

6. The Connection Key Information screen opens. Choose whether to send the connection file in an email or save it to disk (Macintosh users can't send the file in an email from within Dreamweaver; they can only save connection keys to disk, from which they can be manually attached to and outgoing email). Then enter the password or pass phrase for the connection file, repeat the password or pass phrase for verification, and click Next.

Contribute encrypts the connection file with the password or pass phrase so that it can't be opened except by the intended recipient.

7. The Summary screen of the Export Wizard appears, allowing you to review the information. If you need to make changes, click Back. Otherwise, click Done.

8. If you chose to send the connection key by email (again, you only have this opportunity in Windows), Contribute launches your email program and creates a new message with the connection key as an attachment, the subject already filled in, and the instructions in the body of the message. Address the message, make any other changes you want, and send the mail on its way.

or

If you chose to save the connection key to disk, the Export Connection Key dialog appears (**Figure 11.9**). Choose the location on your hard drive or local network for the connection key, and click Save.

Figure 11.9 Macintosh users only have the option to save connection keys to disk; they can't send them via email.

Figure 11.10 On Dreamweaver MX for Windows, you'll find the Site window in the Files panel group.

Figure 11.11 Dreamweaver MX for Macintosh has a stand-alone Site window.

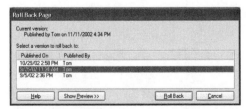

Figure 11.12 The Roll Back Page dialog lets you choose previous versions of your Web pages, which you can then republish to your Web site.

Using Contribute Rollback in Dreamweaver

As detailed in Chapter 3, "Building Web Pages," and Chapter 10, "Site Administration," Contribute has the ability to roll back pages on your Web sites to previously published versions. Site administrators can enable or disable rollback for permission groups of users. Dreamweaver MX can also roll back pages from Contribute users or other Dreamweaver MX users.

You use Dreamweaver's Site window to manage files and folders on your site. Dreamweaver can show the local copy of the site on your machine, as well as the remote copy on the Web server. In this respect it works differently from Contribute, which always browses and accesses files on the server, and makes local copies of pages only when you are working on draft pages.

In the Windows version of Dreamweaver MX, the Site window is part of the Files panel group (**Figure 11.10**). On the Macintosh, the Site window is a stand-alone window but works almost exactly the same way (**Figure 11.11**).

To roll back to a previous page version:

1. In the Site window, on either the local site or the remote site, select the page you want to roll back.

2. From the menu bar at the top of the Site window, choose File > Roll Back Page (Windows), or choose Roll Back Page from the Site pop-up menu (Macintosh).

   Dreamweaver gets the version information for the page from the server and displays the Roll Back Page dialog (**Figure 11.12**). If the page has no previous versions or the previously published version was created outside of Contribute or Dreamweaver, the Roll Back Page dialog tells you.

continued on next page

3. From the list of versions, choose a previous version.

4. (Optional) If you want to confirm that the version you selected is the one you want, click Show Preview.

The Roll Back Page dialog expands to show you the preview (Windows), or the page opens in your system's default browser (Macintosh). If it's not the version you want, select another in the Roll Back Page dialog.

5. Click Roll Back.

Dreamweaver replaces the currently published version of the page with the previously published version.

✔ Tips

■ If you roll back to a previously published version of a page, the current version is saved on the server as a rollback version, and you can revert to it if you wish.

■ Like Contribute, Dreamweaver can roll back "only" 99 versions of a given page, though the prudent site administrator will probably set far fewer rollbacks.

■ Dreamweaver users can roll back pages changed by Contribute users or Dreamweaver users, and pages modified in Dreamweaver can be rolled back by either Dreamweaver or Contribute.

■ If you have a file checked out (using Dreamweaver's check-in/check-out feature), you must check the file in before you can roll it back to a previous version.

■ If someone else has checked the file out (or is editing it with Contribute), you won't be able to either edit it or roll it back until he or she is done and has released the file.

■ Dreamweaver's Roll Back Page dialog is resizable in Windows but not on the Macintosh. On both platforms, however, you can drag the border between the columns to the right or left to make more room for the information in the columns.

CUSTOMIZING CONTRIBUTE

Macromedia Contribute does a fine job straight out of the box, but like many of the Macromedia programs, it can be customized and extended. For example, you can add your own Sample Pages, which contributors can use from the New Page dialog. You can customize Contribute's Welcome screen with your organization's logo. You can modify and rearrange Contribute's menus so that they are more to your liking, and you can add or change the commands on the menus. Similarly, you can customize Contribute's toolbars. And if you have special instructions or tutorials for your users, you can add topics to Contribute's How Do I panel.

Fair warning—geeky stuff ahead: Unlike the operations covered in the rest of this book, customizing Contribute often means working with a text editor; and for most things, you'll need some knowledge of HTML, JavaScript, and XML, and that means getting your hands dirty with some code. On the other hand, there are some quite useful ways you can customize Contribute that require little or no coding, and I'll show you those, too.

A complete discussion of customizing and extending Contribute is beyond the scope of this book, but I'll point you toward some resources that will help if you want to learn more.

Understanding Contribute Extensibility

Like Dreamweaver MX, Contribute's user interface is written in a combination of HTML, JavaScript, and XML. In fact, virtually everything you see and work with in Contribute is an *extension* written in one of these languages and stored in Contribute's Configuration folder (more about that folder later). Contribute can be customized by advanced Contribute users and by site administrators using Dreamweaver MX or a simple text editor, such as Notepad (though you'll probably want a more robust tool). If you're familiar with the extensibility of other Macromedia products, such as Flash MX, Fireworks MX, or especially Dreamweaver MX, you'll find Contribute's extensibility to be familiar but maybe also a bit frustrating. That's because Contribute uses conventions and procedures for extensibility similar to Dreamweaver's, but it is somewhat more limited in scope and, for the end user, is not as convenient as Dreamweaver in this regard.

The standard mechanism for extending other programs in the MX product line is to use the Macromedia Extension Manager, a program that installs prepackaged extensions you download from the Macromedia Exchange site (an online clearinghouse for extensions; you can reach it by choosing Help > Dreamweaver Exchange while in Dreamweaver) or other Web sites. The Extension Manager is necessary because installing the different parts of an extension in the correct places to work with the Macromedia programs can be tricky. Unfortunately, Contribute 1.0 does not support the Extension Manager, although future versions of Contribute probably will. As a result, if you want to customize and extend Contribute, you'll have to do it manually.

You can download *Extending Contribute*, a book in Adobe Acrobat form, from the Contribute Designer and Developer Center, at http://www.macromedia.com/desdev/contribute/. This book details the similarities and differences between extending Contribute and extending Dreamweaver.

It's also possible to create your own extensions, such as dialog boxes, menu commands, and so on, using a combination of HTML, JavaScript, and XML. You'll need a considerable amount of experience using these languages, as well as a good understanding of how Dreamweaver extensions are made. For more information on that lengthy subject, see the online book *Extending Dreamweaver*, which you can access by choosing Help > Extending Dreamweaver from within Dreamweaver MX. You might also find it useful to download *Customizing Macromedia Dreamweaver MX* from the Macromedia Dreamweaver Support Center, at http://www.macromedia.com/support/dreamweaver/.

✔ Tips

- If you need a friendly introduction to JavaScript, I suggest *JavaScript for the World Wide Web: Visual QuickStart Guide, Fourth Edition*, from Peachpit Press, and written by Dori Smith and ... uh ... me.

- You can find more information on HTML in the excellent *HTML for the World Wide Web, Visual QuickStart Guide, Fifth Edition*, written by Elizabeth Castro and also from Peachpit Press. The same author has also written *XML for the World Wide Web, Visual QuickStart Guide* for Peachpit Press.

- If the online resources at Macromedia's Web site aren't available at the specific URLs above, don't panic; companies are forever changing their Web sites, and you might have to search around a bit to find what you want.

Extension folder structure

As mentioned above, Contribute's Configuration folder contains the extensions that come with Contribute. In most cases you will modify files in this folder to customize Contribute.

You'll find Contribute's Configuration folder at C:\Program Files\Macromedia\ Contribute\Configuration\ (**Figure 12.1**).

Inside the Configuration folder, you'll find many other folders, which contain the files that actually make up the extensions. These folders, such as Commands, Menus, Objects, and Toolbars, make it easy to find the particular files you need to modify in order to customize Contribute. For example, to change the names of menus or the shortcut keys associated with menus, you must edit the file ccmenus.xml inside the Menus folder.

— Configuration folder   *Commands —*

Figure 12.1 Contribute's Configuration folder contains all the extensions that make up the program.

What's Extensible?

Contribute allows you to extend the following features in the same way you extend them in Dreamweaver MX:

◆ Menus, including the ones on the menu bar and the shortcut menus. You need to add new menu items to trigger extensions such as objects or commands.

◆ Toolbars, which can be modified by adding or deleting buttons and other controls; you can also define new toolbars.

◆ Commands, which perform specific tasks. For example, any task invoked from a menu or toolbar is a command. By default, new objects appear at the bottom of Contribute's Format menu.

◆ Objects, which can insert blocks of HTML code or text into the current document. For example, you could define an object that would insert boilerplate text into a page. By default, new objects appear at the bottom of Contribute's Insert menu.

◆ Floating Panels, which are similar to commands but can work interactively while the user is editing a page. For example, you can create a floating panel that warns the user when he or she inserts images that are too large.

◆ Translators.

◆ Third Party Tags.

◆ JavaScript Extensions.

Figure 12.2 Begin the process of saving a page as a Sample Page in the Administer Website dialog.

Creating Sample Pages Templates

One of the most useful customizations you can make to Contribute—adding to the set of Sample Pages that come with Contribute—requires no code modifications. All you need is to be the Contribute site administrator.

Sample Pages are pages on the site that serve as models for new pages but don't have locked and editable regions. Instead, the entire page is editable. Basically, a Sample Page is a regular HTML file that Contribute uses as stationery for a new page.

You should be aware that after you add a new Sample Page, it appears in the Templates folder of the New Page dialog, not in the Sample Web Pages folder, which is apparently reserved for Macromedia's use. Your content contributors will be able to choose the new Sample Page you added just as they would choose any other template for your site.

Before you begin the process below, you should have already created the page you want to become the Sample Page in Dreamweaver or Contribute.

To add a Sample Page template:

1. Choose Edit > Administer Websites, then from the cascading menu choose the Web site to which you want to add the sample page.

   The Administrator Password dialog appears.

2. Enter the administrator password, and click OK.

   The Administer Website dialog appears (**Figure 12.2**).

continued on next page

3. In the "Permission groups" section of the dialog, select the group that will use the new Sample Page, and then click Edit Group.

The Permission Group dialog for the selected group appears (**Figure 12.3**).

4. In the category list on the left side of the dialog, click New Pages.

5. In the "Allow users to" section of the dialog, select "Create a new page by copying a page from this list" (**Figure 12.4**).

6. Click Add.

The Choose File on Website dialog appears (**Figure 12.5**).

7. Navigate to and select the page you want to become the Sample Page.

A preview of the page appears in the Preview section of the dialog.

8. Click OK.

You return to the Permission Group dialog, and the page you selected is added to the list box.

9. Click OK to return to the Administer Website dialog.

10. Click OK to save your administrative changes.

To use your new Sample Page, browse to the site where you want to create the new page, choose File > New Page, or click New Page on the toolbar. Your new Sample Page appears in the Templates folder of the New Page dialog.

✔ Tips

■ When you select pages to become Sample Pages, you are restricted to the Web site associated with the permission group you're modifying; you can't choose from pages on other sites for which you have connections. This is different from some other operations in Contribute where you use the Choose File on Website dialog.

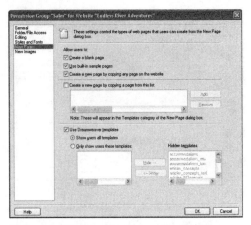

Figure 12.3 Select the New Pages category of the Permission Group dialog.

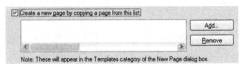

Figure 12.4 Once you select "Create a new page by copying a page from this list," the Add and Remove buttons become active.

Figure 12.5 Choose the file you want to make into a Sample Page.

■ There's no reason why Sample Pages can't be created in Dreamweaver. Saving a template as a Dreamweaver template gives the file a different extension (**.dwt**).

Figure 12.6 Contribute's Welcome screen before any connections have been added.

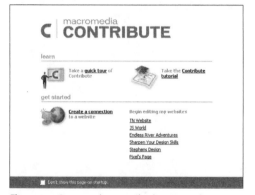

Figure 12.7 Once you have made site connections, your Web sites become available on the Welcome screen.

Customizing the Welcome Screen

You can customize the Welcome screen, the screen that users see when they first launch Contribute. You might want to customize it to reflect the logo of your organization. If you're a designer, you can customize the Welcome screen for your clients.

The Welcome screen looks simple (**Figure 12.6**), but it is actually an automatically generated HTML file (welcome.htm) based on a Dreamweaver template (welcome.dwt). Rather than having the Welcome page be a static HTML page, you can add Contribute connections, and the Welcome page changes to list all your connections (**Figure 12.7**).

To change the Welcome page, you use Dreamweaver to edit the welcome.dwt template, which is located in the Contribute\Configuration\Content\Welcome\ folder. After you edit the template and save your changes, the next time you launch Contribute, it will generate a new welcome.htm file based on the new template.

To customize the Welcome screen:

1. Quit Contribute.

2. On the Windows desktop, open the Contribute\Configuration\Content\Welcome\ folder, and make a duplicate of the welcome.dwt file so that you have a backup in case anything goes awry.

3. Launch Dreamweaver.

4. Choose File > Open, and then open the file C:\Program Files\Macromedia Contribute\Configuration\Content\Welcome\welcome.dwt.

   The file opens in Dreamweaver.

continued on next page

5. Make your changes to the template file, and then save and close the template.

Because the Welcome template is a special template, it doesn't work the way other templates work in Contribute. You should not save it in the Templates folder; instead, save it in the Welcome folder. Any assets for this page, such as CSS files or images, should also be stored in the Welcome folder.

6. Quit Dreamweaver.

7. Launch Contribute.

The new Welcome screen appears (**Figure 12.8**).

✔ Tips

■ If you want multiple users to be able to use your new Welcome page, you must copy the edited `welcome.dwt` template file to each user's `Contribute\Configuration\ Content\Welcome\` folder.

■ For a more detailed and technical discussion of customizing the Welcome screen, look for the article "Co-Branding Contribute" on the Macromedia Contribute Designer and Development Center site.

■ The Welcome screen is one of the features Contribute has that Dreamweaver does not. Another such feature is Contribute's How Do I panel. Like the Welcome screen, it can be customized to allow you to provide online help for your site's users. Because the procedure for modifying the How Do I panel is beyond the scope of this book, I suggest you obtain *Extending Contribute*, from the Contribute Designer and Developer Center on Macromedia's Web site.

Figure 12.8 After you modify the template on which the Welcome screen is based, the Welcome screen gains a whole new look.

```
5  <<XML>> (Menus/ccmenus)
263  <menubar name="Main Window" id="DWMainWindow">
264     <menu name="Apple" id="DWMenu_Apple" platform="mac">
265        <menuitem name="About Contribute..."        command="
266     </menu>
267     <menu name="_File" id="DWMenu_File">
268        <menuitem name="_New Page..."    key="Cmd+N"        d
269        <menuitem name="_Edit Page"      key="Cmd+Shift+E"  fil
270        <separator/>
271        <menuitem name="_Publish"        key="Cmd+Shift+P"  ena
272        <menuitem name="P_ublish as New Page..."       enabl
273        <separator/>
```

Figure 12.9 Here's a close-up of the ccmenus.xml file showing the beginning of the code for the main menu bar.

Customizing Menus

You can change the names of any items in any of Contribute's menus and rearrange the order of items in the menus. Contribute defines all of its menus, including the ones in the menu bar and its shortcut menus, in an XML file called ccmenus.xml, in the Contribute\Configuration\Menus\ folder. To change the menus, you must use Dreamweaver or a text editor to edit the ccmenus.xml file.

Before you change this file, be sure to quit Contribute and duplicate the ccmenus.xml file under another name so that you have a backup in case you make a mistake in your editing.

To change menu items:

1. Quit Contribute.

2. Launch Dreamweaver or whatever text-editing program you use for editing XML files.

3. Choose File > Open, and then open the file C:\Program Files\Macromedia Contribute\Configuration\Menus\ccmenus.xml.

   The file opens in Dreamweaver or your other editing program (**Figure 12.9**). The main menu bar for Contribute is toward the end of the file; you can recognize it because it begins with
   `<menubar name="Main Window"`
   → `id="DWMainWindow">`

   (See the gray arrow in step 3? Because book pages are narrower than computer screens, some of the lines of code in this chapter are too long to fit on the page. When that happens, we've broken the line into segments, inserted the gray arrow to indicate that it's a continued line, and indented the rest of the line. But when you see the line in your text editor, it should be one long line.)

continued on next page

CUSTOMIZING MENUS

4. To move a menu or menu item, select it from its opening tag (example: <menu>) to its closing tag (example: </menu>), cut it, place the insertion point where you want to move it, then paste.

or

To rename a menu or menu item, find it in the code and then change its name attribute.

or

To insert a separator in a menu, enter <separator /> between two menuitem tags.

5. Save and close ccmenus.xml, and then launch Contribute to see your changes.

✔ Tip

■ Do not change the ID attribute of any menu item in the ccmenus.xml file, or Contribute might not be able to perform the menu command.

Syntax of the menus.xml File

The menus.xml file is, like all XML files, a highly structured file. It contains a list of menu bars, menus, menu items, keyboard shortcuts, shortcut lists, and separators. The items are described using XML tags. Here's a simplified syntax for the tags that make up the menus.xml file:

◆ The <menubar> tag provides information about a menu bar in the Contribute menu structure. It must contain a name and ID attribute, and one or more menu tags.

◆ The <menu> tag gives information about a menu or submenu. Its name attribute is the name of the menu as it will appear in the menu bar. It requires an ID attribute. The menu tag can contain one or more menuitem tags and one or more separator tags. If it contains other menu tags, those tags will become a submenu of the parent menu tag.

◆ The <menuitem> tag defines a menu item. It must have name and ID attributes. It can contain the key attribute, which defines the keyboard shortcut for the menu item. A menuitem tag must be contained within a menu tag.

◆ The <separator> tag causes a separator to appear in the menu. It has no attributes and must be contained in a menu tag.

For more details on each of these tags, download *Customizing Macromedia Dreamweaver MX* from the Macromedia Dreamweaver Support Center.

CUSTOMIZING MENUS

Changing Keyboard Shortcuts

You can change keyboard shortcuts for a command if you don't agree with Macromedia's commands.

Before you begin, be sure to quit Contribute and duplicate the `ccmenus.xml` file under another name so that you have a backup in case you make a mistake in your editing.

To change keyboard shortcuts:

1. Quit Contribute.

2. Launch Dreamweaver or whatever text-editing program you use for editing XML files.

3. Choose File > Open, and then open the file `C:\Program Files\Macromedia Contribute\ Configuration\Menus\ccmenus.xml`.

   The file opens in Dreamweaver or your other editing program. The main menu bar for Contribute is toward the end of the file; you can recognize it because it begins with

   ```
   <menubar name="Main Window"
    →id="DWMainWindow">
   ```

continues on next page

Keyboard Command String Equivalents

When assigning keyboard shortcuts, Contribute uses particular strings to denote modifier keys; you use the strings within the key attribute. Because Contribute is derived from Dreamweaver, and Dreamweaver is a cross-platform application, the strings denote different modifier keys on different platforms.

- `Cmd` specifies the Control key for Windows or the Command key for Macintosh.

- `Ctrl` specifies the Control key for either platform.

- `Shift` specifies the Shift key for both platforms.

- `Alt` and `Opt` interchangeably specify the Alt key for Windows or the Option key for Macintosh.

Use the plus sign (+) to separate modifier keys—for example, Cmd+P.

4. If you're reassigning an existing keyboard shortcut (for example, you want to swap the shortcut for Insert Table, which is Ctrl - Alt - T, with that of Select Table, which is Ctrl - T), find the menu item to which the shortcut is currently assigned, and change the key attribute.

For example, you would find the following lines (**Figure 12.10**):

```
<menuitem name="Select Table"
→key="Cmd+T">
```

and

```
<menu name="Insert"
→id="DWMenu_Table_Insert">
<menuitem name="Table"
→key="Cmd+Opt+T">
```

Then you would swap the code between the quotes in the key attributes.

or

If you want to add a shortcut key to a menu item that does not currently have one, add key="" anywhere between attributes inside the menuitem tag. Place the shortcut key between the double quotes.

5. Save and close ccmenus.xml, and then launch Contribute to see your changes.

✔ Tips

■ When changing keyboard commands, make sure you don't accidentally duplicate a keyboard command that is in use elsewhere in the program. If the keyboard shortcut is already being used and you don't remove that use of it, the shortcut will apply only to the first menu item that uses it and will be ignored for the second menu item.

■ Underscores in menu or menu-item names indicate the letter in the name to be used for Windows accelerator keys. I've omitted them in the code samples above for clarity.

```
<menu name="T_able" id="DWMenu_Table">
    <menuitem name="_Select Table" key="Cmd+T"
        <menu name="_Insert" id="DWMenu_Table_Insert">
        <menuitem name="_Table"      key="Cmd+Opt+T">
        <separator />
```

Figure 12.10 These lines in the ccmenus.xml file create the Table menu, the Select Table menu item, the Insert menu item, and the Insert > Table submenu item.

INDEX

128-bit encryption, 158
  character, 170

A

absolute links, 96
access privileges. *See* permissions
accessibility features/standards, 87, 144, 170,
    181–182
Accessibility page, Macromedia, 182
accessible templates, 182
Acrobat files, 145
Active Link color, 44
Add Bookmark command, 29, 123
Address bar, 28
Administer Website dialog
    assigning permissions in, 165
    assigning sitewide settings in, 159
    purpose of, 157
    sending connection keys via email from, 158,
        185
Administer Websites command, 20, 157
administration. *See* site administration
Administrator group, 165
Administrator Information screen, 19
Administrator Password dialog, 157, 159, 164,
    185
administrators
    accommodating multiple, 180–181
    changing contact information for, 159
    contrasted with content contributors, 10
    identifying, 156
    responsibilities of, 11, 155
    setting passwords for, 19, 157, 159–160
    setting up, 157–158
    workflow for, 11

Adobe
    Acrobat, 145
    GoLive, 134
    Photoshop, 88, 89
Album Page template, 36
Align command, 67
alignment
    image, 87
    table, 125, 126
    text, 67
ALT text
    changing, 86
    and Editing permissions, 170
    illustration of, 87
    purpose of, 84, 87
    requiring, 182
AltaVista, 45
alternate Web addresses, 162–163
alternative text, 84. *See also* ALT text
anchors, 107–109
    adding, 107
    copying, 109
    defined, 107
    linking to, 108
    modifying, 109
    purpose of, 107
Arial font, 63
Available Fonts list, 64

B

<b> tag, 170
Back button, 28
background color
    for pages, 42, 44
    for tables, 114, 123
    for templates, 141

background images, 42, 44
_baks folder, 161
bitmap images, 151. *See also* BMP format
_blank target, 99
Blank Web Page option, 32
<blockquote> tag, 68
blue text, 7
BMP format, 84, 151
Bold button/command, 61
bold text, 60, 170
Bookmarks menu, 29
borders
    frame, 47
    image, 87
    table, 113, 114
breaks. *See* line breaks; paragraph breaks
Browse mode, 6
Browse to Link dialog, 102
browser. *See* Web browser
Browser toolbar, 4, 6
bulleted lists, 72, 73
Business templates, 36

C

Calendar templates, 36
Cancel button, 7
Cancel Draft command, 34
Cascading Style Sheets. *See* CSS styles
Castro, Elizabeth, 191
ccmenus.xml file, 197, 198, 199
CD-ROM, Contribute, 3
cells. *See also* tables
    defined, 112
    formatting, 125
    merging/splitting, 127
    padding/spacing for, 113, 114
    selecting, 116
    setting properties for, 128–129
Center button, 67
check-in/check-out name, 183
Check Spelling button/dialog, 80
Choose button, 30
Choose File on Website dialog, 28, 30–31, 153
Choose Folder button, 33
Choose Image on Website dialog, 83
Chosen Fonts list, 64
Clear command, 82, 85
Collaboration templates, 36
collisions, filename, 92
color
    background (*See* background color)
    border, 114
    box, 43

highlight, 66
link, 43, 44, 96
sample page, 36
text, 44
color picker, 43, 66, 123
columns. *See also* tables
    deleting, 121
    inserting, 120
    resizing, 117
    selecting, 116
    sorting, 131
commands. *See also* specific commands
    changing keyboard shortcuts for, 199–200
    extending, 192
Communicator, Netscape, x
companion Web site, xii
computer
    inserting images from, 82
    linking to files on, 105–106
    system requirements, x–xi
Configuration folder, 190, 192
Connection Disabling feature, 25
connection icons, 24
Connection Information screen, 18
Connection Key Information screen, 21
connection keys
    and administrator workflow, 11
    defined, 11
    importing, 23
    protecting, 21, 22
    security considerations, 158
    sending via email, 21–22, 158, 185–186
    setting permissions for recipients of, 20
    sharing, 15, 20–22, 158, 185–186
Connection Wizard, 15–19
    creating site connections with, 17–19
    editing site connections with, 24
    and FTP, 16
    purpose of, 15
    starting, 17
connections, 17–25
    creating, 17–19
    disabling, 25
    duplicating, 24
    editing, 24
    icons for, 24
    removing, 164
    saving to file, 20
    sharing, 20–22
    types of, 19
content contributors, 10, 12
Contribute
    connection choices, 19
    customizing, 189–200

Designer and Developer Center, 191
enabling Dreamweaver settings for, 183–184
extensibility of, 190–192
installing, 3
interface, 4–8
knowledge/skills required for, xi–xii, 1
purpose of, ix–x, xii
registering, 3
running, 3
system requirements, x–xi
using with other programs, 2
Web resources, xii
workflow, 10–13
Contribute Site Settings dialog, 183
contribute.xml file, 160
contributors, 10, 12
Copy command, 59
copyright symbol, 77
Courier font, 60, 63
Create Connection button, 6
Create New Page command, 100
CSS styles
applying, 70–71
clearing, 71
contrasted with HTML styles, 69
displaying full names of, 70
and editable regions, 139
hiding, 171
meaning of acronym, 58
naming, 137, 171
purpose of, 58, 69
Customizing Macromedia Dreamweaver MX,
191, 198

D

Date command, 75
dates
inserting in pages, 75
sorting, 130
default.htm/default.html file, 162
definition lists, 72
Delete Column command, 121
Delete Folder button, 31
Delete Page command, 35, 93
Delete Row command, 121
descriptions, setting page, 45
design. *See* Web design
Design Notes, 164
Designer and Developer Center, Contribute, 191
dictionary, spelling, 80
Directory List option, 73

disabilities, accommodating people with, 87, 144,
170, 181–182
disk space, x
.doc file extension, 151
document window, 4, 5
documents
directory location for, 145
editing imported, 150–154
encoding of, 43, 44
file-size considerations, 147, 148
importing, 143, 145, 146–149
linking to, 143, 147
setting preferences for, 147
splitting large, 147
documents folder, 145
draft pages. *See also* Web pages
exporting as HTML, 56
linking to, 97–99
publishing, 51–52
saving, 48
sending for review, 49–50
spell-checking, 80
Dreamweaver, 177–188
bug fixes, 179
check-in/check-out name, 183
checking version of, 178
connection choices, 19
creating Sample Pages in, 194
customizing, 191
enabling settings for Contribute, 183–184
extensions, 191
FTP client functions, 16
and image replacement, 93
and media files, 94
and page targets, 99
purpose of, 2
recommended book on, 191, 198
sending connection keys from, 185–186
and site administration, 155, 156, 177
and standards compliance, 182
Support Center, 179, 191
and tables, 112
templates, 13, 38–39, 133–141, 182 (*See also*
templates)
updating, 178, 179
using Contribute rollback in, 187–188
.dwt file extension, 136, 194

E

Edit Font List dialog, 64
Edit Image command, 90
Edit Page button/command, 5, 6, 41
editable regions
  and automatic updates, 136
  defined, 38, 134
  identifying, 38, 135, 139
  labeling, 137, 139
  naming, 139
  working in, 139–140
editing
  folders, 11
  frame content, 47
  images, 89–91
  imported documents, 150–154
  links, 110
  offline (*See* offline editing)
  permission groups, 175
  site connections, 24
  text, 58–59
  URLs, 103
  Web pages, 12, 15, 41, 46–47
Editing permissions, 138, 169–170
Editing toolbar, 7, 60, 70
<em> tag, 61, 170
email
  clients, x
  default program for sending, 22
  links, 104
  sending connection keys via, 21–22, 158,
    185–186
  sending draft pages for review via, x, 49–50
Email Review command, 49
Emphasis style, 60, 61. *See also* <em> tag
encoding, document, 43, 44
encryption, 158, 186
Eudora, x
Excel
  AutoFormat option, 122
  creating links to documents from, 143, 145
  file extension, 151
  file-size considerations, 148
  importing documents from, 143, 146–149
  saving documents from, as Web pages, 144
Exchange, Macromedia, 190
Export command, 56
Export Connection Key dialog, 22, 186
Export Wizard, 20–22, 185
Extending Contribute, 191, 196
Extending Dreamweaver, 191
extensibility features, 190–192
Extension Manager, 179, 190

external documents, 143–154
  compatible formats for, 145
  defined, 144
  directory location for, 145
  editing, 150–154
  file-size considerations, 147, 148
  importing, 143, 145, 146–149
  saving as Web pages, 144
  setting preferences for, 147
  splitting large, 147
eyedropper, 66

F

Favorites menu, 29
File Access permissions, 168
File Download dialog, 153
file editors
  adding, 152
  Contribute's preset, 151
  setting preferences for, 89, 152
File on My Computer command, 105
File Placeholder screen, 153
File Transfer Protocol. *See* FTP
filename collisions, 92
files
  automatic renaming of, 92
  controlling access to, 168
  deleting unwanted duplicate, 92
  linking to, 105–106
  naming, 106
Find and Replace dialog, 78–79
Find Source dialog, 90
Fireworks
  compatible file types for, 151
  and image conversions, 84
  and image editing, 89, 90–91
  and resizing of images, 88
Fixed Width style, 60, 61
Flash Movie Properties dialog, 94
Flash movies, 94
Flash Player, 94
floating panels, 192
Folder/File Access permissions, 168
folders
  changing structure of, 31
  controlling access to, 168
  entering paths for, 18
  restricting editing of, 11
font combinations
  changing, 64
  Contribute's preset, 62, 63
  defined, 62

Font Size menu, 62, 63, 171
font styles, 60–61
fonts, 62–64
    allowing users to specify, 171
    choosing, 63
    HTML size limitations for, 62
    setting size of, 63
    Web browser considerations, 62, 63
Fonts permissions, 138, 171
Forest sample pages, 36
Format menu, 60, 70
Format Table dialog, 122, 124
formatting
    tables, 122–124, 125
    text
        with CSS styles, 69–71, 137
        with HTML styles, 60–68
Forward button, 28
frames
    defined, 46
    editing content in, 47
    red border around, 47
    selecting, 47
    ways of using, 46
framesets
    copying pages containing, 40
    creating/editing, 46
    defined, 46
    and page-review process, 50
FTP, 16, 18
FTP screen, Connection Wizard, 18

G

General Content template, 36
General permissions, 167
Georgia font, 63
GIF format, 84, 151
Go To Web Address dialog, 28, 29
GoLive, 134
Google, 45
graphic formats, 84. *See also* images
green outline, 38, 135, 139
Group Information screen, 21
group permissions. *See* permission groups
Grouped Item List template, 36

H

handles
    resize, 117
    selection, 88
hard disk

linking to files on, 105–106
    space required on, x
hardware requirements, x–xi
headers, table, 114
Heading styles, 65
Help window, 9
Helvetica font, 63
Highlight Color button/command, 66
Home Page template, 36
Home Pages pop-up menu, 30, 31
horizontal rules, 76
hot spots, 95
How Do I panel
    customizing, 189, 196
    illustration of, 8
    location of, 4
    purpose of, 8
    resizing, 8
HREF field, 98, 99, 103
`.htm/.html` file extension, 33, 162
HTML
    exporting draft page as, 56
    font-size limitations, 62
    and frames/framesets, 46
    recommended book on, 191
    saving as template, 136
    styles, 60–68, 139
    table format, 111
    tags (*See* specific tags)
    viewing, 55
HTML for the World Wide Web, 191
HTML validator, W3C, 182
hyperlinks, 7, 95. *See also* links

I

`<i>` tag, 170
IE. *See* Internet Explorer
image-editing programs, 84, 88
Image Properties dialog, 86, 87
images, 81–93
    adding borders around, 87
    adding to pages/templates, 82–84, 138
    adjusting properties of, 86–87
    aligning, 87
    constraining proportions of, 87
    converting, 84
    copying and pasting, 84
    deleting from pages, 85
    directory location for, 85
    dragging and dropping, 84
    editing, 89–91
    limiting size of, 173
    overusing, 81

images *(continued)*
    providing ALT text for, 84, 87
    purpose of, 81
    replacing, 92–93
images, continued
    resizing, 87, 88
    Web-ready formats for, 84
images directory, 85
Import Connection Key dialog, 23
importing
    connection keys, 23
    Excel documents, 143, 146–149
    Word documents, 145, 146–149
Indent button/command, 68
Index and URL Mapping dialog, 163
index page, 162–163
index.htm/index.html file, 162
info bar, 6, 7, 141
Insert Column button, 119
Insert Date dialog, 75
Insert Link dialog, 97, 99, 100, 104, 110
Insert menu, 60
Insert Other Character dialog, 77
Insert Row button, 119
Insert Rows or Columns dialog, 120
Insert Table dialog, 112
Installer, Contribute, 3
Internet. *See also* Web
    connecting to, x
    search engines, 45
Internet Explorer
    changing settings for, 5
    contrasted with Contribute's browser, 29
    and document window, 5
    Favorites menu, 29
    version required for running Contribute, x
Internet Properties control panel, 22
Italic button/command, 61
italic text, 61, 170

J

JavaScript, 189, 190, 191, 192
JavaScript for the World Wide Web, 191
JPEG format, 84, 151
Justify button, 67

K

keyboard shortcuts
    for alignment, 67
    for browser navigation, 28
    changing, 199–200

modifier keys for, 199
keys, connection
    and administrator workflow, 11
    defined, 11
    importing, 23
    protecting, 21, 22
    security considerations, 158
    sending via email, 21–22, 158, 185–186
    setting permissions for recipients of, 20
    sharing, 15, 20–22, 158, 185–186
keywords, setting page, 45

L

language encoding, 43
LANs, x, 15, 16
Latin alphabet, 43
layouts
    importing complex, 148–149
    using tables for, 111, 113
Left button, 67
line breaks, 59, 170
Link color, 44
links, 95–110
    absolute *vs.* relative, 96
    choosing colors for, 43, 44, 96
    creating, 33, 37
        to draft pages, 97–99
        to email addresses, 104
        to local files, 105–106
        to section anchors, 107–109
        to Web addresses, 102–103
    creating new pages from, 100–101
    editing, 110
    identifying, 7
    parts of, 95
    removing, 110
    types of, 96
List Properties dialog, 73
lists
    creating, 72
    nesting, 74
    purpose of, 72
    setting properties for, 73
    types of, 72
local area networks. *See* LANs
Local/Network connections, 16, 18
locked regions
    and automatic updates, 136
    defined, 38
    examples of, 38
    identifying, 39, 134
    including Print button in, 138
    purpose of, 134

"Look in" pop-up menu, 31
Lotus Notes, x
Lucida Grande font, 64

M

Mac OS X, xi
Macintosh
    and Dreamweaver, xi, 178
    fonts, 63, 64
    modifier keys, 199
Macromedia
    Accessibility page, 182
    Contribute (*See* Contribute)
    Dreamweaver (*See* Dreamweaver)
    Exchange, 190
    Extension Manager, 190
    Fireworks (*See* Fireworks)
    Flash movies, 94
    registering program with, 3
    Web site, 94, 178
mailto links, 104
Manage Extensions command, 179
margins, setting page, 43
media files, 81, 94
Meeting Notes template, 36
memory requirements, x
Menu bar, 4
<menu> tag, 198
<menubar> tag, 198
<menuitem> tag, 198
menus
    adding shortcut keys to, 200
    customizing, 192, 197–198
    underscores in, 200
menus.xml file, 198
Merge Cells command, 127
META tags, 45
Microsoft
    Excel (*See* Excel)
    Internet Explorer (*See* Internet Explorer)
    Office, 144, 145, 147, 148
    Outlook/Outlook Express, x
    Paint, 84, 151
    PowerPoint, 145, 151
    Windows (*See* Windows)
    Word, 143 (*See also* Word documents)
_mm folder, 160, 175
mmhide prefix, 171
modifier keys, 199
monitors, x
Month templates, 36
MP3 files, 94, 145

Multiple-Photo template, 36
My Connections dialog
    editing site connections in, 24
    enabling Web sites in, 160
    identifying site administrator in, 156
    importing connection keys in, 23
    making site connections in, 17
    removing administration in, 164

N

named anchors, 107
naming
    CSS styles, 137, 171
    editable regions, 139
    files, 106
    index pages, 162
    menus/menu items, 198
    permission groups, 174
    templates, 136
    Web pages, 32, 33, 51
navigation shortcuts, 28
navigation tool, 8
nested lists, 74
nested tables, 112, 113
Netscape Communicator, x
New Document dialog, 182
New Folder button, 31
New Images permissions, 173
New Page button/command, 6, 32, 36, 38, 135
New Page dialog, 32, 37, 39, 135, 172
New Pages permissions, 172
No cursor, 39
nonbreaking space character, 170
Normal style, 65
Notepad, 147, 151, 152, 190
numbered lists, 72, 73
numbers, sorting, 131

O

objects, extending, 192
Office 2000/XP, 144
Office applications, 144, 145, 147, 148
offline editing, 15, 41, 134. *See also* Work Offline
    command
onscreen help, 9
orphan pages, 32
OS X, xi. *See also* Macintosh
Outdent button/command, 68
Outlook/Outlook Express, x

P

<p> tag, 58, 169
padding
    cell, 113, 114
    image, 87
Page Keywords and Description dialog, 45
page margins, 43
"page not found" error message, 162
Page Properties button/command, 42, 96
page titles, 32, 39, 42
page-versioning system, 178. *See also* rollbacks
pages. *See* Web pages
Pages panel
    illustrations of, 8, 33
    location of, 4
    purpose of, 8
    resizing, 8
Paint, Microsoft, 84, 151
paragraph breaks, 58, 169
paragraph spacing, 169
passwords
    administrator, 19, 157, 159–160
    and built-in browser, 29
    connection key, 21, 22
    FTP, 18
Paste command, 59
PC, running Contribute on, x–xi. *See also*
    Windows
Permission Group dialog, 166, 194
permission groups
    and administrator workflow, 11
    assigning permissions to, 165–166
    creating, 11, 174
    deleting, 176
    duplicating, 176
    editing, 175
    facilitating creation of, 180
    joining, 174
    naming, 174
    removing single user from, 176
    setting home page for, 167
    sharing, 20
    and template access, 136
    and text styles, 138
Permission Sets feature, 20
permissions, 165–176
    and administrator passwords, 19
    assigning, 165–166
    categories
        Editing, 138, 169–170
        Folder/File Access, 168
        General, 167
        New Images, 173

New Pages, 172
        Styles and Fonts, 138, 171
    defined, 11, 155
    storage of settings for, 156
Personal templates, 36
Photo Album Page template, 36
Photoshop, 88, 89
placeholders
    file, 153
    image, 82
    table, 126
Places pane, 91
Player, Flash, 94
PNG format, 84, 151
point sizes, font, 62
port numbers, 163
Portable Network Graphics, 151. *See also* PNG
    format
PowerPoint, 145, 151
.ppt file extension, 151
preferences
    for external documents, 147
    for file editors, 89, 152
    for invisible elements, 107
    for number of undo steps, 85
    for section anchors, 107
Presentation Slide template, 36
Preview in Browser command, 55
Print Preview command/dialog, 54
printing, creating style sheet for easy, 138
privileges. *See* permissions
production servers, 15
Project Home Page template, 36
properties
    cell, 128–129
    Flash movie, 94
    horizontal rule, 76
    image, 86–87
    list, 73
    section anchor, 109
    table, 125–126
    template, 141
    Web page, 42–44
Publish As New Page command/dialog, 48, 52
Publish button, 7
Publish New Linked Pages dialog, 51
Publish New Page dialog, 33
Publish/Publish All commands, 51

Q

Qualcomm Eudora, x
QuickTime files, 94

R

RAM, x
RDS connections, 19
Redo command, 59
Refresh button, 29
registration, program, 3
Rehabilitation Act, 144
relative links, 96
Remove Link command, 110
repeating regions, 140
Replace/Replace All buttons, 78, 79
Report template, 36
resize handles, 117
Résumé template, 36
Retry Connection button, 25
Right button, 67
Roll Back Page command/dialog, 53, 187–188
Roll Back to Previous Version command, 53
rollbacks
  and administration removal, 164
  changing number of, 161
  defined, 53
  enabling, 161
  maximum number of, 53
  using in Dreamweaver, 187–188
rows. *See also* tables
  deleting, 121
  duplicating, 140
  formatting, 125
  inserting, 119, 120, 140
  resizing, 118
  selecting, 115
rules, horizontal, 76

S

Sample Pages
  accessibility of, 182
  categories of, 36
  color choices for, 36
  creating, 193–194
  creating new pages from, 36–37, 101, 194
  defined, 134, 193
  folder for, 101, 193
  preventing access to, 172
  purpose of, 13, 27
  and standards compliance, 182
Sample Web Pages folder, 101, 193
Save As command, 52
Save command, 48
Save for Later button, 7
screen shots, xi

search engines, 45
Section Anchor dialog, 107
section anchors, 107–109
  adding, 107
  defined, 107
  linking to, 108
  modifying, 109
  purpose of, 107
Section508.com, 144
Select a Frame to Edit dialog, 47
Select Connection Key dialog, 23
Select File dialog, 105
Select Image dialog, 82
selection handles, 88
_self target, 99
Send Connection Key button, 20
<separator> tag, 198
servers
  connecting to, 15–16 (*See also* Connection
    Wizard)
  types of, 15
shared settings file, 156, 160, 175
shopping carts, online, 29
shortcuts
  alignment, 67
  browser navigation, 28
  changing, 199–200
  modifier keys for, 199
sidebar, 8
Silver sample pages, 36
site administration
  removing, 164
  using Dreamweaver for, 155, 156, 177
site administrators
  accommodating multiple, 180–181
  changing contact information for, 159
  contrasted with content contributors, 10
  identifying, 156
  responsibilities of, 11, 155
  setting passwords for, 19, 157, 159–160
  setting up, 157–158
  workflow for, 11
site connections, 17–25
  creating, 17–19
  disabling, 25
  duplicating, 24
  editing, 24
  icons for, 24
  removing, 164
  saving to file, 20
  sharing, 20–22
  types of, 19
Site Definition dialog, 184
site structure, Contribute-friendly, 180–181

sites. *See* Web sites
Sitewide Settings dialog, 159, 161, 164
Size command, 63
Sky sample pages, 36
Smith, Dori, 191
Sort Table dialog, 131
sorting algorithm, 130
source code
    allowing users to modify, 138
    viewing Web page, 45, 55
source documents, 145
SourceSafe Database connections, 19
special characters, 77, 106
spelling checker, 80
Split Cell dialog, 127
spreadsheets. *See* Excel
staging servers, 15
standards compliance, 181–182. *See also* Web
        standards
Strikethrough style, 60, 61
Strong style, 60, 61
<strong> tag, 61
Style menu, 65, 70
styles
    allowing users to apply, 138, 171
    CSS, 58, 69–71, 137, 139
    HTML, 60–68, 139
Styles and Fonts permissions, 138, 171
Summary screen
    Connection Wizard, 19
    Export Wizard, 21
symbols, 77
system requirements, x–xi

T

Table Data template, 36
Table Properties dialog, 117, 118, 125, 128
tables, 111–131
    as alternative to indenting, 68
    anatomy of, 114
    creating, 112–114
    deleting rows/columns from, 121
    formatting, 122–124, 125
    inserting rows/columns in, 119–120, 140
    as layout devices, 111, 113
    merging/splitting cells in, 127
    nesting, 112, 113
    removing, 121
    removing background colors from, 123
    repeating regions, 140
    resizing, 117–118
    saving, 123, 124

    selecting elements in, 115–116
    setting properties for, 125–126, 128–129
    setting width of, 113
    sorting contents of, 130–131
    tagging headers in, 114
    Web browser considerations, 118
tabular information, 111. *See also* tables
"Target frame" pop-up menu, 99
targets, 99
Template Properties dialog, 141
templates. *See also* Sample Pages
    allowing/preventing access to, 136, 138, 172
    and automatic page updates, 136
    choosing, 134, 135
    creating, 134, 137–138
    creating pages from, 38–39, 101, 134–135
    Dreamweaver vs. non-Dreamweaver, 13, 134
    editable regions in, 38, 134 (*See also* editable
        regions)
    file extension for, 136
    locked regions in, 38, 134 (*See also* locked
        regions)
    purpose of, 13, 133, 136
    renaming, 136
    setting properties for, 141
Templates folder, 136, 193
test servers, 15
text
    aligning, 67
    alternative, 84, 86 (*See also* ALT text)
    coloring, 44, 66
    copying and pasting, 59
    editing, 58–59
    finding and replacing, 78–79
    formatting
        with CSS styles, 69–71, 137
        with HTML styles, 60–68
    highlighting, 66
    indenting, 68
    wrapping, 118, 125, 129
text-alignment buttons, 67
Text Color button/command, 66
text files, 151
<th> tag, 114
TIF format, 84
Times New Roman font, 63
titles, page, 32, 39, 42
tool tips, 87
toolbars
    illustrations of, 6, 7
    location of, 4
    modifying, 192
_top target, 99
trademark symbol, 77

translators, 192
Trebuchet font, 63
tutorials, 8
Two-Column template, 36
.txt file extension, 151

U

Underline command, 61
Undo command, 53, 59, 110
Undo Image command, 85
Uniform Resource Locators. *See* URLs
Up One Level button, 31
updater, Dreamweaver, 178, 179
updates, automatic, 136
URLs. *See also* Web addresses
  changing mapping for, 163
  copying and pasting, 103
  editing, 103
  meaning of acronym, 95
  purpose of, 95
  typing in browser Address bar, 28
User Information screen, 17
Users group, 165

V

Verdana font, 63
versions, rolling back pages to previous, 53, 161,
  187–188
Visited Link color, 44
Visual QuickStart Guides, 191

W

WAV files, 94
W3C HTML validator, 182
Web addresses
  linking to, 102–103
  sending visitors to alternate, 162–163
  for specific sites
    Accessibility page, 182
    companion Web site, xii
    Contribute Designer and Developer Center,
      191
    Dreamweaver Support Center, 191
    Macromedia, 94, 178, 182, 191
    Section508.com, 144
    Web Standards Project, 144
Web browser
  changing settings for, 5
  Contribute's built-in, 5, 28–29

font considerations, 62
previewing pages in, 55
table considerations, 118
Web design
  programs, 2
  updating, by changing template, 136
  using images/media files in, 81
Web pages. *See also* Web sites; specific page
    elements
  allowing coworkers to review, 49–50
  automatic updating of, 136
  browsing, 28–31
  canceling new/draft, 34
  copying, 40
  creating, 13
    from Dreamweaver templates, 38–39, 101,
      134–135
    with New Page command, 32–33
    from Sample Pages, 36–37, 101
  creating links for, 33, 37, 97–99 (*See also* links)
  deleting, 35
  editing, 12, 41, 46–47, 57–59
  exporting as HTML, 56
  laying out elements on, 111
  locking portions of, 13
  naming, 32, 33, 51
  organizing content on, 72
  previewing in external browsers, 55
  printing, 54, 138
  publishing, 33, 51–52
  rolling back to previous versions of, 53, 161,
      187–188
  saving drafts of, 48
  setting keywords/descriptions for, 45
  setting properties for, 42–44
  spell-checking, 80
  using frames in, 46
  viewing source code for, 45, 55
Web sites. *See also* Web pages
  adding pages to, 32–33
  addresses for specific (*See* Web addresses)
  allowing users to change/update, ix–x
  browsing, 28–31
  building Contribute-friendly, 180–181
  building standards compliance into, 181–182
  changing folder structure for, 31
  connecting to, 17–19
  deleting pages from, 35
  increasing complexity of, ix
  inserting images from, 83
  removing administration from, 164
  standards-based, 144
Web standards, 144, 181–182

Web Standards Project, 144
WebDAV protocol, 19
Website Home Page screen, 17
Welcome screen, 3, 189, 195–196
Western (Latin1) encoding, 43
Windows
    fonts, 63
Windows, continued
    modifier keys, 199
    system requirements, x
Windows Media files, 94, 145
Word documents
    editing, 150
    file extension for, 151
    file-size considerations, 147, 148
    importing, 145, 146–149
    linking to, 143, 145, 146
    page-layout considerations, 148–149
    saving as Web pages, 144
    setting preferences for, 147
    splitting large, 147
word processing, 58
Work Offline command, 25, 41, 158
Work Online button, 25
workflow
    for contributors, 12
    defined, 2
    for site administrator, 11
worksheets, 149. *See also* Excel
World Wide Web. *See* Web
"Wrap text" box, 118, 129
wrapping, text, 118, 125, 129

X

.xls file extension, 151
XML
    and connection keys, 158
    and Contribute customization, 189
    and Contribute extensibility, 190
    file editor, 151
    recommended book on, 191
    tags, 198
XML for the World Wide Web, 191

Y

Yahoo! Search, 45